DEMOCRATIC DECENTRALISATION AND THE POSITIONING OF INDIGENOUS

Books by the Same Author

- Tribal Development and inclusive Policy (2018)

About the Editor

Prof. Nupur Tiwary is currently the Chair Professor of Dr. Ambedkar Chair in Social Justice of Indian Institute of Public Administration (under the aegis of Dr. Ambedkar Foundation, Ministry of Social Justice and Empowerment). She had also worked as Special Director, National Tribal Research Institute (under the aegis of Ministry of Tribal Affairs, Government of India, New Delhi and Head, Centre of Excellence (CoE) for Tribal Affairs, (MoTA) at Indian Institute of Public Administration IIPA, New Delhi. Earlier, she had worked as Senior Consultant to the former Union Minister of Panchayati Raj, providing inputs on Local governance. She was also a faculty member at LBSNAA, Mussoorie, she has lectured vastly in India and abroad.

Her current research interests include Social Justice, Tribal Development, Tribal Local Governance, Tribal Public Policy, Gender Policy and Governance, Left Wing Extremism, Rural Development and Decentralization. She has authored Fifty-five research papers/articles, published in peer reviewed National and International journals. She has authored seven books and four Monographs and has contributed Chapters in eleven volumes. She has published eighty reports for Government of India.

As the head of the Centre of Excellence, Tribal Affairs, she had mentored 5000 Tribal Ph.D. scholars under the NFST Scheme of M/o Tribal Affairs, Government of India. For this purpose, she has conducted various programmes to improve the quality of research to enable doctoral scholars to participate in multiple research and evaluation activities undertaken at the Central and State levels. These programmes also identify scholars for their entrepreneurial skills and capacity.

She has been the Project Director of eleven major projects, in recent times. commissioned by the Government of India. She has also Worked on Five Major Projects, funded by international bodies, i.e. IDRC, Irish Aid, UNDP, and also Union Ministry of Panchayati Raj, Ministry of Rural Development, and UNDP.

She has been a member of fourteen Expert committees constituted by Government of India. She was the Domain Expert for PM award for excellence in Public Administration (2014).
She regularly appears on national news television in various panel discussions as an expert on various developmental issues (DD News, Rajya Sabha, Samsad TV, ZEE TV, and other media. She has travelled vastly to the USA, France, Germany, Switzerland, Belgium, Sweden, Netherlands, Holland, Thailand, Vietnam, Malaysia, UAE. She has lectured widely in India and Abroad.

DEMOCRATIC DECENTRALISATION AND THE POSITIONING OF INDIGENOUS

From Margins to Mainstream

Edited by

Nupur Tiwary

CONCEPT PUBLISHING COMPANY PVT. LTD.
NEW DELHI - 110 059

ISBN: 978-93-6344-601-4

First Published 2024

Published and Printed by

Concept Publishing Company Pvt. Ltd.
A/15-16, Commercial Block, Mohan Garden
New Delhi-110059 (India)
T: +91-11-41101460
E: publishing@conceptpub.com, *W*: www.conceptpub.com

Cataloging in Publication--Courtesy: D.K. Agencies (P) Ltd. <docinfo@dkagencies.com>

Democratic decentralisation and the positioning of indigenous :
from margins to mainstream / editor, Nupur Tiwary.
pages cm
Contributed articles.
"... brought out by Dr. Ambedkar Chair in Social Justice, IIPA, New Delhi"--Preface.
Includes bibliographical references and index.
ISBN 9789363446014

1. Decentralization in government--India. 2. Democracy--India. 3. Tribal government--India. 4. India--Scheduled tribes--Legal status, laws, etc. 5. Rural development--India. I. Tiwari, Nupur, editor. II. Indian Institute of Public Administration. Dr. Ambedkar Chair in Social Justice, issuing body.

LCC JS7009.D46 2024 | DDC 320.80954 23

Preface

It gives me immense pleasure that the book 'Democratic Decentralisation and the Positioning of Indigenous' is brought out by Dr. Ambedkar Chair in Social Justice, IIPA, New Delhi. This book will help researchers and administrators understand the challenges to decentralization and tribal mainstreaming for sustainable development. Today, more than ever, countries are actively engaged in developing decentralization programmes to make their public administration more effective, flexible, and responsive. In 2000, the World Bank estimated that between 80-100 per cent of the world's countries were experimenting with some form of decentralization of governance system. This book presents the work done on decentralization—keeping tribal local self-governance at the centre of analysis—by compiling the work of researchers and experts who are well-versed in the domain of decentralization and tribal welfare and understand its nuances. Their research would inevitably help develop policy-level interventions and reforms to strengthen the foundation of tribal local self-governance and consequently help achieve sustainable development for the tribal communities. This book explores four specific themes. The first theme focuses on the challenges to decentralization and tribal development in India. It tries to address the question of compatibility between tribal development and decentralization—if and how both are contiguous to each other. The theme explores how the concept of decentralization emerged in the governance model in India and eventually assesses its impact on state capacity and political stability.

The subsequent theme brings forward the remarkable work and rigorous research done on tribal self-governance and tribal development—in areas of health, education, and access to government schemes designed explicitly for tribal communities. The overarching motive, apart from understanding the work of the researchers, is to use the empirical findings and present them in an accessible form to policymakers, development practitioners, and the broad spectrum of student communities from different disciplines.

The concept of decentralization takes many forms and extends to several dimensions by encompassing institutional restructuring. Decentralization occurs when the Central Government disperses responsibility for fiscal, political, and administrative importance to its regional branch offices. The third theme of the book talks about fiscal decentralization—which determines the responsibilities of imposition and collection of taxes, incurring public expenditure. Fiscal decentralization, in essence, rectifies the vertical imbalance in governance. It helps achieve growth and equity in different regions in India by giving due importance to the unique demography of the country.

The fourth and final theme provides a close analytical view of the impact of the PESA Act, 1996 in enabling tribal local self-governance and promoting tribal development. The Centre enacted the Panchayat (Extension of the Scheduled Areas) Act, 1996 or PESA, to ensure self-governance through Gram Sabhas (village assemblies) for people living in scheduled areas. The Act legally recognizes the right of tribal communities and residents of the scheduled areas, to govern themselves through their systems of self-government and also acknowledges their traditional rights over natural resources.

Overall, all the research papers have covered myriad topics related to decentralization and tribal local self-governance, demonstrating the correlation between the applicability of PESA in the tribal areas. This will demonstrate to us how the implementation of PESA can shape the socio-cultural circumstances of tribal communities. The researchers have done a commendable appraisal of the administrative structure of the past 35 years.

The pace of development and progress in tribal areas concerning economic development and social justice has comparatively been slower than in the rural non-tribal regions in India. Therefore, the tribal communities deserve greater attention to their unique problems, which, without contestation, should align with their customs and traditions. The growth of India's tribal communities should be imagined from foundational and deliberation levels itself. For this to happen, the rights vested to the Gram Sabhas in villages should be realistic and not simply reflected on paper. Gram Sabhas should be better informed about their rights and should exercise them for the development of the tribal community. There should be a particular focus on the issues of tribal communities, and priority should be given to the implementation of welfare schemes and programmes that address their multidimensional issues. This is only possible when we develop a deep understanding of the reality of tribes in India and the problems they face. Mere growth of the economy cannot bring social justice and balanced development unless it is coupled with poverty alleviation and employment-generating opportunities for the deprived and marginalized sections of the society. If circumstances removing poverty and destitution are mitigated, only then more space can be generated to develop a programme that addresses the pressing issues such as education, health, skill development, and nutrition for the tribal communities. And this is possible when we take into account the reality of tribes in India with respect to their development and inclusion. This book intends to bring together the work done on tribal development by re-imagining their role in self-governance.

Prof. Nupur Tiwary
Chair Professor
Dr. Ambedkar Chair in Social Justice,
IIPA, New Delhi

Acknowledgements

The editor would like to thank Concept Publishing Company Pvt. Ltd. for their unfailing support in publishing this book. This book would not have been possible without the consistent involvement of the Dr. Ambedkar Chair in Social Justice, Indian Institute of Public Administration (IIPA).

The book's editor would like to extend her sincere gratitude to the contributors who have consented to provide their research papers for compilation and helped to make this book. Their work in their respective domains has expanded the book's scope and made it comprehensive. The editor sincerely regards Midhila Mallika and Abinash Kumar, whose broad knowledge of democratic decentralization and strengthening of state has been an asset in making this book. Dr. Pushpender Yadav's study on the role of Panchayats and the impact of Swachh Bharat Abhiyan in tribal villages has been very influential. The editor sincerely thanks Muzafer Rasool Hajam, Dr. Manvendra Singh, Rubaya Akther, Dr. Meena Rani, Dr. Kanhaiya Lal, Vikram Prashant, Umesh Kumar and Tavseef Ahmad Mir, for their research papers that present crucial insights about the impact of decentralization of state. This book would have been incomplete without the invaluable contribution of Saurabh Bharne, Dr. Manvendra Singh, Priya Dahiya, Rinki Dahiya, Rukmini Bhattacharjee, and Nayakara Veeresha. Their papers have explored myriad dimensions of fiscal decentralization in India. The editor is grateful for the contribution of Shivani Tiwari, Abhishek Sarta, Sandeep Tripathi, and Dr. Pushpendra Yadav. They have extensively researched the role of PESA in land acquisition in India.

Lastly, the editor thanks all the researchers and scholars for their active involvement, who helped put this together, and put their efforts into bringing this book to completion.

Prof. Nupur Tiwary
Dr. Ambedkar Chair in Social Justice,
IIPA

Contents

List of Contributors

Abhishek Sarta, Research Scholar, Department of Public Administration, Panjab University, Chandigarh.
Email: kksarta@gmail.com

Abinash Kumar, Assistant Professor, Department of Political Science, Rajendra Memorial Women's College (Magadh University), (Bihar).
Email: abinash.abinash.kumar48@gmail.com

Kanhaiya Lal, Assistant Professor, Department of Political Science, S.S. Memorial College, Ranchi University, Ranchi (Jharkhand).
Email: kanhaiyal14@gmail.com

Manvendra Singh, Associate Professor, Department of Governance & Public Administration, Lovely Professional University, (Punjab). **Email:** manvendra.21755@lpu.co.in

Meena Rani, Assistant Professor of Public Administration, University of Rajasthan, Jaipur (Rajasthan).
Email: drmeena82@gmail.com

Midhila Mallika, Ph.D. Research Scholar, CSSEIP Centre for the Study of Social Exclusion and Inclusive Policy, Jawaharlal Nehru University, (New Delhi). **Email:** midhilamallyka@gmail.com

Muzafer Rasool Hajam, Ph.D. Research Scholar, Department of Government & Public Administration, Lovely Professional University (Punjab). **Email:** shinestar793@gmail.com

Nayakara Veeresha, Ph.D. Research Scholar, Centre for Political Institutions, Governance and Development (CPIGD), Institute for Social and Economic Change (ISEC), Dr. VKRV Rao Road, Nagarabhavi, Bengaluru (Karnataka).
Email: nayakaraveeresha@gmail.com

Priya Dahiya, Assistant Professor, Jesus and Mary College, University of Delhi, (New Delhi).
Email: priyadse102@gmail.com

Pushpender Yadav, Assistant Professor, Maulana Azad National Institute of Technology, Department of Humanities and Social Sciences, Bhopal (Madhya Pradesh).
Email: pushpender1@gmail.com

Rinki Dahiya, M.Phil, Research Scholar, University of Delhi, (New Delhi). **Email:** rinkydahiya95@gmail.com

Rubaya Akther, Ph.D. Research Scholar, Department of Governance & Public Administration, Lovely Professional University (Punjab). **Email:** rubayagull9@gmail.com

Rukmini Bhattacharjee, Amity University, Kolkata, (West Bengal). **Email:** rukminibhattacharjeekolkata@gmail.com

Sandeep Tripathi, Research Scholar, Department of Humanities and Social Sciences, Maulana Azad National Institute of Technology, Bhopal (Madhya Pradesh).
Email: sandeeptripathi1998@gmail.com

Saurabh Bharne, Research Scholar, Department of Humanities and Social Sciences, Maulana Azad National Institute of Technology, Bhopal (Madhya Pradesh).
Email: saurabh.bharne@gmail.com

Shivani Tiwari, Research Scholar, Department of Humanities & Social Sciences, Maulana Azad National Institute of Technology Bhopal (Madhya Pradesh). **Email:** tsshivani10@gmail.com

Tavseef Ahmad Mir, Ph.D. Scholar, Department of Governance and Public Administration, Lovely Professional University, (Punjab). **Email:** mir.tavseef@rediffmail.com

Umesh Kumar, Department of Public Administration, Veer Kunwar Singh University, Ara (Bihar).

Vikram Prashant, Research Scholar, Department of Public Administration, Veer Kunwar Singh University, Ara (Bihar).
Email: vikprashant89@gmail.com

Introduction

Decentralization is at the centre of policy reform agenda worldwide. Today, more than ever, countries are actively engaged in developing decentralization programmes to make their public administration more effective, flexible, and responsive. In 2000, the World Bank estimated that between 80-100 per cent of the world's countries were experimenting with some form of decentralization of governance system. This book presents the work done on decentralization—keeping tribal local self-governance at the centre of analysis—by compiling the work of researchers, policy-makers, and experts who are well-versed in the domain of tribal welfare and understand its nuances. Their research would inevitably help develop policy-level interventions and reforms to strengthen the foundation of tribal local self-governance and consequently help achieve sustainable development for the tribal communities.

The first theme focuses on the challenges to decentralization and tribal development in India. It tries to address the question of compatibility between tribal development and decentralization—if and how both are contiguous to each other. The theme explores how the concept of decentralization emerged in the governance model in India and eventually assesses its impact on state capacity and political stability. In her chapter "Historical Subjugation and Democratic Decentralisation: The positioning of Indigenous Elected Women Representatives in Governance Participation of Wayanad, Kerala",

Midhila Mallika presents a detailed understanding of the indigenous population of Wayanad, the district constituting the highest tribal population in Kerala. Her chapter discusses how the manifestation of historical oppression influences decentralisation at the grassroots level and tribal development and further assesses its impact on the devolution and delegation of decentralised power among indigenous women. Saurabh Bharne and Dr. Pushpender Yadav contribute to the research on tribal affairs with their seminal chapter on "Multicultural Decentralisation in India: An Experience with Asymmetric and Multi level federalism for integrating Northeast Tribal Groups". The chapter assesses the arrangements made for ethnic groups of the north-east to protect their cultural identities through self-government, in order to their better accommodation in the polity and examines the Indian experience with the asymmetric and multilevel federalism in the North-east to strengthen the Indian state and to provide it stability. Abinash Kumar studies Panchayati Raj Institutions of Bihar in general and Nawada district of Bihar in particular. His chapter "Decentralization and the Strengthening of the State: A Case Study of Province of Bihar" delineates the dynamics of decentralization and the shortcomings of functioning of Panchayats in Bihar and argues that democratic and substantive decentralization can strengthen the institution of the state.

The subsequent theme brings forward the remarkable work and rigorous research done on tribal self-governance and tribal development—in areas of health, education, and access to government schemes designed explicitly for tribal communities. The overarching motive, apart from understanding the work of the researchers, is to use the empirical findings and present them in an accessible form to policy-makers, development practitioners, and the broad spectrum of student communities from different disciplines. In their comprehensive research work on "Decentralization, Inclusive Development and Impact of Smart City Mission in Srinagar City of Jammu & Kashmir", Muzafer Rasool Hajam, Dr. Manvendra Singh and Rubaya Akther explore in-depth the Srinagar Smart City Mission, which aims to bridge the socio- economic divide in the region's urban landscape by emphasizing on socio-economic and political empowerment of vulnerable urban communities including slum dwellers, street vendors, daily-wage labourers, artisans, widows, and senior citizens. The chapter also suggests measures to revive good governance and inclusive development approaches to ensure citizen-centric and responsive administration.

The concept of decentralization takes many forms and extends to several dimensions by encompassing institutional restructuring. Decentralization occurs when the Central Government disperses responsibility for fiscal, political, and administrative importance to its regional branch offices. The third theme of the book talks about fiscal decentralization—which determines the responsibilities of imposition and collection of taxes, incurring of public expenditure. Fiscal decentralization, in essence, rectifies the vertical imbalance in governance. It helps achieve growth and equity in different regions in India by giving due importance to the unique demography of the country. The chapters presented under this theme explore the structure of decentralization in India and its impact on mitigating poverty, addressing the concerns of stark inequality, and the participation of people in local self-governance. In her work "The Dynamism of Decentralization from the Perspective of 'Suppleness' of the Strong States—A Theoretical Study Rukmini Bhattacharjee shows how the presence of decentralization in the system of administration redefines the idea of the state and deepening democracy. In her chapter "Decentralization and the Supple State: An Indian Experience", Dr. Meena Rani analyses how decentralization helps in making a 'supple state' and discusses how systematically planned decentralization would enable in forming a strong state. Delving deep into the subject of "Decentralization through Local Self Governance in Pulwama, Jammu and Kashmir." Tavseef Ahmad Mir and Dr. Manvendra Singh attempt to study the process of decentralization through local self-governance in the Pulwama and suggest pertinent measures to improve the participation of local people through decentralization. In "Challenges to Decentralisation and Tribal Development: A study of state of Himachal Pradesh" Abhishek Sarta captures the challenges to decentralisation in the tribal areas of Himachal Pradesh. The chapter highlights important issues related to the socio-economic development of tribals in the state of Himachal Pradesh, while also noting the steps taken by the Government of

Himachal Pradesh for the sustainable development of tribal areas and various policy implications. In her chapter "Decentralization and Selected issues in local–level fiscal decentralization" Rinki Dahiya analyzes fiscal decentralisation in India and its impact on the provision of basic services.

Dr. Kanhaiya Lal presents his case about why decentralization needs to be more effective in promoting the activities of Panchayati Raj Institutions increasing the provision of resource allocation in states in his research study "Challenges of Decentralization in Rural Development." Through their study on "Challenges to Decentralisation and Tribal Development through E-governance", Vikram Prashant and Umesh Kumar provide an overview about how E-governance can contribute to tribal development and decentralization of power. In this connection, their chapter reviews the various plans and policies of E-governance that are implemented in the tribal areas and their impact on tribal development. Nayakara Veeresha's research paper on "PESA and Self-Governance in Fifth Schedule Areas: Role of Governor" establishes the existence of astrong correlation between the applicability of PESA, low human development indicators and vulnerability to extreme or radical politics, thus implying that efficient and effective implementation of PESA goes a long way in dealing with socio-political uprisings and helps deepen participatory democracy.

The fourth and final theme provides a close analytical view of the impact of the PESA Act, 1996 in enabling tribal local self-governance and promoting tribal development. The Centre enacted the Panchayat (Extension of the Scheduled Areas) Act, 1996 or PESA, to ensure self-governance through Gram Sabhas (village assemblies) for people living in Scheduled areas. The Act legally recognizes the right of tribal communities and residents of the Scheduled areas, to govern themselves through their systems of self-government and also acknowledges their traditional rights over natural resources. Sandeep Tripathi's and Dr. Pushpender Yadav's "How PESA had failed in ensuring "Mava Nate Mava Raj (Our Village Our Rule)"? studies how legislations like PESA have failed in preventing the pauperization of tribals leading them to a state of shelterless and assetless destitution. Shivani Tiwari's and Dr. Pushpender Yadav's chapter on "Land Acquisition in

India: Unfurling Panchayats (Extension to Scheduled Areas) Act, 1996 as a Saviour of Scheduled Areas" discuss how PESA plays a central role in Land Acquisition and restoring the traditional right over their resources to the indigenous people. In "Role of village Panchayats and the Swachh Bharat Abhiyan in Tribal villages: A Study of Barwani district in Madhya Pradesh, Dr. Pushpender Yadav highlights the impact of Swachh Bharat Abhiyan programme and issues which are still prevailed in the tribal rural villages.

Overall, all the research chapters have covered myriad topics related to decentralization and tribal local self-governance, demonstrating the correlation between the applicability of PESA in the tribal areas. This will demonstrate to us how the implementation of PESA can shape the socio-cultural circumstances of tribal communities. The researchers have done a commendable appraisal of the administrative structure of the past 35 years.

The pace of development and progress in tribal areas concerning economic development and social justice has comparatively been slower than in the rural non-tribal regions in India. Therefore, the tribal communities deserve greater attention to their unique problems, which, without contestation, should align with their customs and traditions. The growth of India's tribal communities should be imagined from foundational and deliberation levels itself. For this to happen, the rights vested to the Gram Sabhas in villages should be realistic and not simply reflected on paper. Gram Sabhas should be better informed about their rights and should exercise them for the development of the tribal community. There should be a particular focus on the issues of tribal communities, and priority should be given to the implementation of welfare schemes and programmes that address their multidimensional issues. This is only possible when we develop a deep understanding of the reality of tribes in India and the problems they face. Mere growth of the economy cannot bring social justice and balanced development unless it is coupled with poverty alleviation and employment-generating opportunities for the deprived and marginalized sections of the society. If circumstances removing poverty and destitution are mitigated, only then more space can be generated to develop a programme that addresses the pressing issues such as education, health, skill development, and nutrition for the tribal communities.

And this is possible when we take into account the reality of tribes in India with respect to their development and inclusion. This book intends to bring together the work done on tribal development by re-imagining their role in self-governance.

Nupur Tiwary

1

Historical Subjugation and Democratic Decentralisation

The Positioning of Indigenous Elected Women Representatives in Governance Participation of Wayanad, Kerala[1]

Midhila Mallika

If the tribe is an area of exploration, then their contextual argument in building the study in a historical perspective should not be a conjecture. The identity of indigenous communities is revealed and determined by their culture, and lineage along with their geography. Andre Beteille defines a tribe "as an ideal state, a self-contained unit which constitutes a society in itself."[2] Without a deliberate account of history, a tribal community cannot be entirely studied since history is the cornerstone which frames them who they are. The Scheduled Tribes (STs) are the ethnic minority groups in Kerala; they constitute around 1.45 per cent of the total population, with a population close to five lakh.[3] Kerala accounts for 1.5 per cent of the total residents and 0.5 per cent of the total Scheduled Tribe population in India, according to the 2011 Census.[4] There are 36 Scheduled Tribe Communities in Kerala, and each group possesses a distinct identity.[5] The long years of interventions by the State have had a marginal impact on their socio-economic conditions. But still, they are the most disadvantaged section among the significant outlier and marginalised communities in Kerala. It is the bygone suppression and slavery in the hands of settlers, landlords, and the British, resulted in their marginalisation. This historicity of oppression has also minimized the participation and representation of their women in local governance (Scheduled Tribes). However, neither the theoretical studies nor empirical analysis provides definitive evidence that the participation of indigenous women in decentralisation process often positions their role in the Panchayati Raj functioning's based on their historical oppression.

In Kerala, it the northern district Wayanad which has the highest concentration of tribal population. It is the least populated district with a population of 817,420 and it ranks first in Scheduled Tribe population (18.5% of its population) among the districts of Kerala.[6] The indigenous population of Wayanad belongs to different ethnic stocks and has a diverse economy, history, belief system, and practices. Which positions the various tribes of the community in different strata resulting in differential distribution of power in the democratic decentralisation. Mainstreaming women through gender-specific policies is an acknowledged pre-condition for achieving meaningful development in any developing country like India. Recent legislative measures have made possible the greater participation of women in local government. However, there are structural and other constraints that keep some women from actively participating in local governance. Thus, the respective paper discusses how the manifestation of historical oppression influences decentralisation at the grassroots level and tribal development and how it impacts the devolution and delegation of decentralised power among indigenous women within different communities by enhancing the stability and the strengthening of local governance institutions among them.

For the term 2015-2017, Wayanad Panchayat had a total of 429 elected representatives from 23 Gram Panchayats. Among them, 79 men and 49 women represent the indigenous communities.

Paniya, Malaaraya, Adiya, Ulladan, Wayanadankaadar, Karimpalan, Kaatunayka, Kutrichoya, Kuruma/Mullukuruma, Vettakuruma, and Thachinadan Moopen are the indigenous communities existing in Wayanad.[7] Even after the affirmative actions of the 73rd Amendment for STs' in Wayanad Gram Panchayats, all the existing indigenous communities failed to represent themselves in the Panchayats. Among the 12 indigenous communities, Kurichiya and Kuruma's represents more whereas the Paniya, Adiya, Mullukurumaba, and Thachinadan Moopen are in a ratio of 3:5:1.

The Historical Subjugation and the Positioning of Indigenous Women

Women are a group that functions as a vital agent of social cohesion and development in all societies. "They are the largest vulnerable extended group" and are mostly excluded from positions of power even if they constitute half of the population in the world. It is a striking fact that 70 per cent of the total poor in the world are women. The advantages of women being in local bodies are that they can effectively function in recognition of local needs, less possibility of mistakes, check upon bureaucracy, and direct contact with people.[8] When the study says how the locus of women in politics has changed positively due to the intervention of the 73rd Constitutional Amendment Act,[9] for instance, the increase in the number of women sarpanches in the Gram Panchayat of Punjab[10] and the significant roles performed by women in the Panchayat Raj of Karnataka.[11] It is imperative to understand whether the 'quantitative' rise in the representation of women they have gained through reservation in the political decision-making process has translated into 'qualitative' changes in their governance participation is a challenging proposal to discourse.

Since one of the critical academic assessments of the position of marginalized women in PRIs proves that they are lagging behind due to societal restrictions. Women are being used as rubber stamps. Hindrances are from the stage of filing of nominations for females up till the completion of her tenure. During elections, corruption, violence, and even rape cases have been noticed, which shows the traditional masculine concept that holds females back to the four walls of their houses.[12] And if the women are characterized with specific societal identities, such as class, caste, race, ethnicity, then the intensity of troubles are doubled.

Even though the Panchayati Raj system made it possible for the historically marginalised women to participate actively in the governance process at the grassroots level, despite the changes, the societal positioning of these marginalised communities by the mainstream society is still dominating the decision-making process.[13] Indigenous communities, historically marginalised, needed to be studied methodically since they sustain unique customs and habitats and are firmly rooted in self-governance. The studies explaining the importance of deliberation of the Bhuria Committee regarding the indigenous community to identify how the recommendations have affected the reservation concept of the Extension Act acclaim how it is crucial to learn about the indigenous society.[14] Thus, it is essential to study the indigenous society to understand their empowerment through democratic decentralisation.

In India, tribal women have a significant role in the co-management of their natural, social, and economic resources. However, they still suffer a lot; they are backwards due to a traditional outlook, illiteracy, superstition, submissive role in decision-making, social evils, and many other cultural factors. Thus, it is essential to analyse the effects of community racial diversity, local government institutions, and the social capital to identify their governance participation and empowerment.[15]

Kerala is a very dynamic and politically active society, but the state still has a long way to go in becoming socially inclusive. The tribes and fisherfolk are excluded from the so-called development model of Kerala. The conditions of these communities are not a part of this model. As they have not benefited from it, they constitute the Outliers who stand on the margins.[16] As a society where inequality in income and economic opportunities keeps widening, even if there is poverty reduction, cannot be inclusive. An inclusive democracy should ensure dignity for all.[17]

Only an empowered and active citizenry can progress towards social equality and hence even if the process of change at local levels of governance in India is slow, women's increased participation in panchayats is an important part of creating an active citizenry that includes both men and women and challenges the dominant relations of social power.[18] The entry into politics depends on a whole lot of variables like age, occupation, income etc., and the factors such as religion, income, party membership, and occupation also matter. The influence of the party is strong during elections; while it plays an insignificant role in motivating women into politics. Those factors which help women to enter as panchayat members are personal qualities and party support. Moreover, the nature of political orientation and involvement in the social organization also enable them to make inroads to the political pinnacle at the grassroots level.[19] But whereas for elected indigenous women, besides the factors mentioned earlier, other socio-historic factors also result in their marginalities.

Among the twelve indigenous communities, only Kurichiya, Kuruma, Paniya, Adiya, Mullukurumba, and Thachinadan Moopen represented each indigenous community of Wayanad in the Gram Panchayats. The names given to some of these communities are according to their historical positioning. The word, Paniya[20] means worker and Adiya[21] means slave. They believe that these names are attributed to them by their feudal landlords who made them slaves. The term Kurichiya[22] is connected with their historic battle with Pazhassi, and the output is credited to Pazhassi by Kurichiyas. The inferiority they find in accepting names like Paniya and Adiya displays that these titles have not emerged from their self-understanding.

As Kunhaman notes, even the category names conveyed their inferior status in society and as he argues the etymology of names in India gives insight into the traditional social structure. However, in the study, if the State is the protagonist, the term used is a tribe or tribal people, and when the people become the central character, the term used is Adivasi, and when used to explain the different views, their category names like Paniyas and Kurichiyas are used.[23]

In the Wayanad context, it is observed that clear demarcation between them and us merge when Adivasi describe non-Adivasi especially when they describe their marginality and exploitation from the dominant non-Adivasi society. It does not mean that they are isolated from the dominant society. They continuously interact with the non-Adivasi society in their day-to-day living. However, in India for years Adivasi lived in the forest, and no authority can deny their right over forest and land by written documents. As elsewhere in India, in Wayanad also the Adivasi land where they buried their ancestors and the land they protected as sacred groves became the private property of non-Adivasi people. Their territories are also claimed by the State in the name of wildlife sanctuaries, reserved forests or development projects such as plantations. Today, their most crucial need is a collective as well as an individual identity to achieve their lost culture, land, forest and power to self-determination and the same goes for Wayanad.

In Wayanad, with a historical and political consciousness, tribal communities call themselves Adivasi in contrast to non-Adivasi fellow human beings who migrated into their homelands. At the same time, each Adivasi group considers their gothram (clan) unique and tries to maintain the purity of the clan through customary practices integral to their clan. For instance, Paniyas have their ritual practices different from those of Kurichias. When Janu, the Adivasi leader in Wayanad formed Adivasi Gothra Mahasabha an organisation engaged in fighting for land rights, she recognised this diversity as a distinct gothram alongside their assertive unity to fight against the forces that marginalise them. Even though each group has its customs and rituals, Janu asserts: All our songs, customs and medical practices were born from the system of life that we adopted as intimately related to the earth.[24]

The Pollution and Purity among the Indigenous Communities: The caste order in India is amidst the world's bygone forms of surviving social stratification. Indigenous people in Kerala are no different, the established caste sentience and practise prevailed among them positions particular tribe in each stratum of the society. Such as; Kurichiya (landed-land owning agriculturalist), Mullu Kurumbar (land-owning agriculturalist community), Kaatunaiykar (food gatherers), Adiyan (landless agricultural labourers) and Paniya (landless labourers). These divisions with definite consciousness empanel the caste distinction among tribes, but yet there are no sociological rationale why certain tribes would not be acknowledged as castes; resulting tribal studies and its biases specific in recording its most evolutionary conventions.[25]

The notion of untouchability among Brahmins and Shudras is a well-known fact, whereas the caste system among the tribes is a less discoursed area. But there is caste-based marginality among them. Paniyas in the plains of Wayanad experienced severe untouchability within their communities. Since they were classified as the bonded slave tribe, further Adiyas. Historically, they had to keep themselves distant from others to observe clan purity. Some records narrate this exploitation within the tribe originated by the advent of settlers to Wayanad.[26]

The land, caste and bondage are intertwined one proceeds to another for instance; the strong connection between caste hierarchy and land ownership[27] resulted in janmikudiyan vyavastha.[28] The higher caste and those with the possession of land used the lower caste (landless) for the production of capital. Their labour was exploited creating various classes of communities among the tribal society. Paniyas, Adiyas are considered as the polluted community among the tribes because of the work they have performed and that positions them in the lower strata. There was social stratification in the organisation of work among the tribes and it is accounted that other than the notion of pollution practices they were never abused. Kurichiyas custom of clan purity does not lead to the exploitation of the lower community for production and Kuruma respected the rights of the lower caste, even though they both practised untouchability.[29] The Adivasi communities of Wayanad rigorously obeys conventional practices of customs and beliefs. From birth to death, they have rituals that differentiate each tribe from the other.

Conclusion

Tribal societies are the most marginalised segment of Indian society. The relative isolation from the mainstream development process affirmed a constant profuse custom of a well-knit, cohesive social construct and value system backed by their own practices and traditions. They also have diverse indigenous customary institutions to resolve their disputes and regulate their resources and socio-political life.[30] When the new panchayat raj institution was proposed to be included in the tribal domains, it was considered imperative to protect tribal communities from marginalisation in the wake of globalisation. The Ninth Five Year Plan working group[31] recommended introducing participatory planning as vital for the equitable growth in tribal areas, which had not augmented considerable importance since Independence's development process. To strengthen the grassroots-level local bodies and implement the self-rule of tribal areas, Part IX of the Constitution of India, which administers with panchayats, was specifically extended through an act of parliament called the Panchayats Extension to Scheduled V Areas Act (PESA).

Tribal councils among the Adivasi communities are inevitable in the study of their history. The affirmative measure introduced by the Panchayati Raj institutions gave them a voice to represent them in the broader governance machinery. But the indigenous methods of their governmentality are proportionately imperative to their tribal hegemony. Tribal sovereignty prevails and facilitates them the power to govern themselves. The presence of a community leader often functions as a panchayat president among the tribal councils. Among tribals, there are specific functions a Moopen/Adivasi head performs that a panchayat president does not.

But the association of tribal governance system with democratic decentralisation because of the historical oppression experienced by the indigenous communities of Wayanad have positioned them in the marginalities. The largest representation of Kurichiya and Kuruma communities in the Wayanad Grama Panchayats and even after being the highest populated tribal community of Wayanad Paniya being less in representing their community following Adiya and others are the reason for the oppression.

Notes

1. Some of these aspects in detail and at length have been discussed in my doctoral dissertation submitted to Jawaharlal Nehru University on December 2021.
2. Andre Beteille (1986). "The Concept of Tribe with Special Reference to India, *European Journal of Sociology*, Vol. 27, No. 2, pp. 293-318.
3. Economic Review 2016, "Social Service: Welfare of Scheduled Castes, Scheduled Tribes, Other backward Classes and Minorities," State Planning Board, Government of Kerala.
4. *Source*: Census 2011, Office of the Registrar General, India.
5. Kerala Institute for Research Training and Development Studies of Scheduled Castes and Scheduled Tribes (KIRTADS), Tribals in Kerala, Government of Kerala.
6. Kerala, Census of India 2011. 'District Census Handbook Wayanad; Villages and Town-wise Primary Census Abstract (PCA)', Series 33, PART XII-B. Census report—Wayanad Handbook, Kerala: Directorate of Census Operations.
7. Wayanad Grama Panchayat, 2019–20 Varshika Padathi.
8. Amin R and Shelina Akhter, "Women participation in local government and social integration in rural Bangladesh," In Workshop on Enlarging Citizen Participation and Increasing Local Autonomy in Achieving Societal Harmony held in Beijing, PRC by Network of Asia-Pacific Schools and Institutes of Public Administration and Governance (NAPSIPAG) Annual Conference, 2005, pp. 5-7.
9. Tilak D. Gupta, "Breaking into a Male Stronghold—The Panchayat Act Makes it Mandatory to Reserve Seats for Women", *The Telegraph*. July 9, 1994, pp. 15-17.
10. Virender Kaur and Sukhdev Singh (2002). "Role of women members in Panchayati Raj system in Punjab," *Social Action*, p. 50.

11. Devaki Jain (2002). "Building budgets from below," Gender Budget Initiatives, Strate.
12. Samrat Sinha (2007). The Political Empowerment of Minority Women through Panchayati Raj Institutions: A Critical Assessment of India's Experiment with Affirmative Action, Third International Congress, Asian Political and International Studies Association (APISA), New Delhi.
13. Craig Johnson. Priya Deshingkar, and Daniel Start (2003). *Grounding the state: Poverty, inequality and the politics of governance in India's Panchyats*, Overseas Development Institutue (ODI).
14. S.K. Singh (1997). "Self-Governance for the Scheduled Areas," *Journal of rural development*, Hyderabad, pp 601-16.
15. Mohamad Awais 2009). Tosib Alam and Mohamad Asif, "Socio-economic Empowerment of Tribal Women: An Indian Perspective," *International Journal of Rural Studies*, Vol. 16, No. 1, pp. 2-11.
16. John Kurien (1995). "The Kerala model: Its Central Tendency and the Outlier," *Social Scientist*, pp. 70-90.
17. M.A. Oommen and D. Shyjan, "Local Governments and th Inclusion of the Excluded: Towards a Strategic Methodology with Empirical Illustration," *Working Paper* 458, Centre for Development Studies, Thiruvananthapuram, 2014.
18. Shirin M. Rai (2007). "Deliberative democracy and the politics of redistribution: The case of the Indian Panchayats," *Hypatia*, Vol. 22, No. 4, pp. 64-80.
19. Manu Bhaskar (1997). "Women Panchayat Members in Kerala: A Profile," *Economic and Political Weekly*, Vol. 32, No. 17, pp. WS13–WS20.
20. Paniya are the largest tribal community in Kerala, they are the agricultural labourers classified as 'Aborigines-Predial, slaves.' Paniyas were also known for their bravado and recklessness in the past. As a result, they were frequently used/employed as thieves (Keane, 2011). They are the most backward in every path, having witnessed a profound history of slavery in the state. They are a marginalised minority in Kerala who own minimal land and have few niceties (Nair, 1911).
21. Adiyan was believed to be derived from Adiyan or Adiyalar or Adima which indicates a lowest position and slave in Malayalam language. It was also opined by some scholars that, the name originated from the rule of keeping six feet distance with the other upper caste landlords.

22. Kurichiya is the community known for its marital tradition, occupies an important place among the tribes of Kerala. The most ancient and considered as one of the advanced tribal communities in Kerala. They are the only tribe in Kerala who have ownership of land, and also have participation in the political process and in institutions like gram panchayat and many members in this community have joined political parties (Nair, 1911).
23. M. Kunhaman (1982). "Bonded Labour in Kerala among the Hill Tribes of Wayanad," *State and Society*, Vol. 3, No. 2, pp. 50-55.
24. Bhaskaran (2004). Personal/Political, Mother Forest: The Unfinished story of C.K. Janu. (Translated from Malayalam by N. Ravi Shanker), New Delhi: Kali for Women and Women Unlimited.
25. A. Aiyappan (1973). *The Paniyas: An Ex-Slave Tribe of South India*, Calcutta: Institute of Social Research in Anthropology.
26. P.K. Balakrishnan (1983). *Jathivyavasthithiyum Keralacharithravum (malayalam).* Thiruvananthapuram: D.C. Books.
27. Ajith (2002). *Bhoomi Jati Bandhanam* (Malayalam), Kochi: Kanal Prasidhekarana Kendram.
28. Feudal Landlord System.
29. Darley Jose Kjosavic and N. Shanmugaratnam, Property Rights Dynamics and Indigenous Communities in Highland Kerala, South India: An Institutional-Historical Perspective, Modern Asian Studies, Cambridge University Press, 2007.
30. Yatindra Singh Sisodia (2005). "Panchayat Raj in Tribal Regions of Madhya Pradesh", in, Yatindra Singh Sisodia (ed.) *Functioning of Panchayat Raj System*. Jaipur: Rawat Publications.
31. Working Group of 1996.

2

Multicultural Decentralization in India

An Experiment with Asymmetric and Multilevel Federalism for Accommodating Northeast Tribal Groups

Saurabh Bharne and *Pushpender Yadav*

Introduction

The long strives for an independent Indian state from the British colonial rule finally paid off in mid-20th century, when the British government announced their intentions to transfer the power in the particular colony to the Indian hands. However, the governing powers were not transferred to a single Indian administration, as the unfortunate event of partition led to the birth of two nations viz., India and Pakistan. Where Pakistan turned out to be the Islamic Republic, Indian leadership decided to establish the country on the Secular-Democratic formula. The chosen path posed several challenges to the Indian leadership as they had a challenging task of accommodating and administering a vast ethnic diversity into a single Liberal-Democratic polity. Also, as the predominant narrative and trend of that time suggested cultural heterogeneity as a threat for the Nation-State, ensuring unity and integrity simultaneously with the nation-building process in the newly formed Indian state seemed to be an arduous job.

"India is the second-most populous country (population now over a billion) after China, and socially and culturally the most diverse in the world" (Bhattacharya, 2003). India's proverbial demographic diversity can be identified by distinguishing it under the major categories formulated on the basis of religious, language, caste, race and tribe. The population of some of these identified groups, for example, caste groups, is dispersed over the Indian territory, and they live in different parts of the region, whereas the ethno-lingual groups and tribal groups have a long history of residing on their particular territories where they form the majority. The groups living together over a particular territory have a history of some kind of autonomy and self-governance too, as they have been governed under the regional decentralized units before the Indian independence (Bajpai, 2019).

Right from the time of independence, just accommodation and management of the diversity into the Indian polity has been a critical responsibility of Indian leadership. "When India gained independence in 1947, the policy-makers and the framers of the Constitution took cognizance of its multivalent diversity and deliberated on a framework that would provide for a unified but culturally diverse nation-state" (Mahajan, 2006). In doing so, they adopted a legal-plural system where they not only provided an equal recognition and protection to all the cultural and ethnic groups residing here, but also considered some special measures and the affirmative action for the recognized groups and communities, to facilitate their accommodation in the Indian polity. Due to such bold initiatives of acknowledging the minority rights and valuing cultural diversity which defied the dominant thinking of its time, many scholars believe that India provides a prescient model of multiculturalism, as the theoretical discourse of multiculturalism emerged a decade after the adoption of such principles.

To deal with the anxieties of the various minority groups regarding their cultural protection, as well as to ensure the representation and emancipation of the vulnerable minority groups, the policies of group-differentiated rights, including legal pluralism in religious family law and the affirmative action for Scheduled Caste and tribal minorities in the form of reserved seats in legislatures, government jobs, and educational institutions, were enshrined in Constitution of India. However, the major difficulty which Indian leadership encountered in the respective process of eliminating conflict through diversity management was in dealing with the ethnic groups' demands of territorial autonomy and self-governing rights through statehood based on their identity and culture, which they declined in the constituent assembly deliberations by arguing that it might have led towards separatist tendencies (Bajpai, 2019). Later, the simultaneous movements based on such demands compelled the leadership to rethink defining the sub-national units on ethno-regional and linguistic basis, and as a consequence, various new states formed over the next several years. The drawing lines of state on the ethno-regional and linguistic demands and attaching them with the policy of democratic decentralization was seen more or less effective in minimizing the ethnic discords and accommodating the country's major linguistic and ethnic diversity more effectively into the polity.

Multicultural Decentralization in India

"Since independence, federalism—and an ongoing federalizing process which politically accommodates ethnic identity—has remained the most effective method of management and resolution of conflicts" (Bhattacharya, 2003). Also, intertwining the process of granting statehood to several territorially based ethnic identities with democratic decentralization since 1950s, resemble India as a multicultural federation. It was seen as one of the most effective factors behind surviving the Indian democratic state. It resulted positively in the management and resolution of ethnic conflicts and provided for a multinational federal polity.

In the early years of Indian independence, many scholars have expressed their skepticism over the survival of such a vast multi-ethnic country as a nation-state in the conditions of underdevelopment, poverty and regional disparities. Atul Kohli, who has expressed a similar concern in his previous articles, later acknowledged India as a successful functioning democratic state in his book "*The Success of India's Democracy*". According to Kohli, the success of India's democracy can be attributed to the "moderate accommodation of group demands, especially demands based on ethnicity and some decentralization of power" (Kohli, 2001).

However, affirmation of statehood to ethno-regional communities of the Northeast region and ethno-lingual communities of the rest of India took different forms. The creation of constituent units/states based on linguistic identity in India (excluding northeast and few other states) followed the pattern of symmetric decentralization, whereas, in granting special status to the northeastern states, or the sub-units having sizeable number of tribal communities, the formulas of "multilevel" and "asymmetric" federalism dominated.

Asymmetric and Multilevel Federalism in Northeast Region

The diversity of tribal communities has been given special attention in the context of protecting cultural diversity in India. Thus, these communities were provided special rights for governing themselves according to their "customary law and distinct social and religious practices" in the "Scheduled Areas", in addition to the special representation to ensure that they are not entirely isolated from the Indian polity. The Fifth and Sixth Schedules to the Constitution of India deal with the administration and governance of identified Scheduled Areas. Where the former provides for the establishment of "Tribal Advisory Councils" to advise Governor on matters regarding the welfare and amelioration of the Scheduled Tribes in the Scheduled Areas except in the states of Assam, Meghalaya, Tripura and Mizoram, the latter provides for the various "autonomous regional councils" in the aforementioned four north-eastern states. During the initial days of India's independence, the north-eastern region was reluctant to accept the Indian suzerainty. The Indian leadership paid great attention in dealing with the interests of the tribal people of the region. A Sub-Committee was formed to report on the North-East Frontier (Assam) Tribal and Excluded Areas where the self-governance provisions for them were highly supported. Also, Nehru advised the Chief Ministers in his "Letters to Chief Ministers" in the early 1950s to not "to treat them by some single formula because they differ greatly among themselves. It seems obviously undesirable to deny them some kind of self-government or autonomy" (Nehru, 1986). Nehru felt that India should be a sign of protection and liberation for them, and the people living in this area should feel free to live their own lives according to their wishes and genius. The northeast region experienced multicultural decentralization in the 1970s and 1980s when major state reorganization took place there to render autonomy to the different territory rooted ethnic communities. "Special status accorded to identified states, or regions within a state, where the Scheduled Tribes were present in significant numbers, took the form of 'multilevel' and 'asymmetric' federalism" (Arora, 1995). The latter means that all the sub-national units in a federal polity do not enjoy similar powers but some, due to their socio-cultural needs and political history, possess special rights and power. For instance, the Constitution of India, through Article 371, clauses A and G, provide special rights to the states of Nagaland and Mizoram in governing themselves according to their distinct "social practices, customary laws, and community control over ownership and transfer of land and its resources." Apart from the vast tribal heterogeneity in the Northeast region (approximately 600 different tribes) which have been living on a specific territory for a long period, a sizeable number of non-tribal also have a long history on that land. Such cases where vast internal diversity coexists and have contending claims over the territory, need a distinct type of framework, as the formula of rendering separate constituent units to each cultural community may result in unsustainable constituent units. Thus, with the aim to deal with the identity-based ethnic conflict among the culturally distinct minority communities and to accommodate their demands, India experimented the multilevel federal approach. "Multilevel federation entails the creation of, what might be called, sub-federation: a separate structure of governance along with powers to deliberate on issues that contribute to the distinctiveness of a cultural community" (Mahajan, 2005). It provides a framework where certain rights are provided to the territorially concentrated minorities in a region to govern themselves on the central matters in their survival as a distinct cultural group. It states for a kind of dual membership where the community exists as a separate entity in a specified area, but it remains a member of the constituent unit/state for purposes of participation and representation. In India, another level was adjoined in the governmental structure in the form of Regional District Councils, whereas the states constituted the federal units in the polity. This approach is a little broader in accommodating the interests of all the communities residing in a particular territory. Taking the example of the Bodo territorial council, where non-Bodos are in the majority, there are five seats open for all and five reserved for the non-tribals, out of the total of forty-six seats. Also, the Governor of the state of Assam has given the responsibility to fill the six seats by nomination from the unrepresented communities of the Bodoland Territorial area districts. This kind of institutional arrangement has later extended to the other regions of India too, such as Gorkhaland in West Bengal, where it was contemplated viable in accommodating the assertive demands coming from the communities residing there. However, the success of this institutional arrangement varied in different parts, but it worked as a better framework in accommodating the diverse communities minimizing the ethnic discord somehow.

Conclusion

"India was among the first few democracies to embark on the multicultural path. At a time when Western liberalism advocated neutrality and difference-blind approach, India acknowledged the rights of minorities and valued cultural diversity" (Mahajan, 2005).

Such initiative by Indian leadership can surely be considered as innovative and bold as they rejected the ethno-national approach even in the tough situation when charged communal passions arose after the partition of India in 1947, followed by the communal riots. At that time, they dealt with the dual problems of fighting with the arising demand for a Hindu centred polity on the one hand and legitimizing the Constitution in people's minds on the other. Also, the pattern of rendering self-governing rights to the various ethno-regional and linguistic communities through statehood, based on their identity and culture, in negotiating with their demands over the time since independence, resembles India as a multicultural federation. This pattern not only worked in minimizing the ethnic discord, but also "was a shift from the belief that affirmation of particularistic identities in the political sphere would fragment the country and suggested, at least implicitly, that in the case of ethnic and linguistic identities, cultural and political boundaries could overlap without dividing the country" (Mahajan, 2005). The major innovation of the Indian system is the approach of "asymmetric" and "multilevel" federations, which have shown significant success in dealing with the assertive demands of autonomy coming from the distinct communities residing on the same territory and contending claims over it. Overall, the Indian experiment in the process of diversity management resulted in suggesting that "the policy of recognizing culturally distinct groups and creating institutional structures that enable them to govern themselves, can be a way of building loyalties and support for the nation-state" (Mahajan, 2005), and thus predates the multicultural notion as the predominant narrative of that time was suggesting diversity affirmation as a threat to the nation-state.

References

Arora, B. (1995). "Adapting Federalism in India: Multilevel and Asymmetrical Innovations". In B. A. Verney (Ed.), *Multiple Identities in a Single State: Indian Federalism in a Comparative Perspective*. Delhi: Konark Publisher.

Bajpai, R. (2019). Multiculturalism in India An Exception? In R.T. Bevir (Ed.), *Multiculturalism in the British Commonwealth: Comparative*

Perspectives on Theory and Practice (pp. 127-149). California: University of California Press.

Bhattacharya, H. (2003). Multiculturalism in Contemporary India. *International Journal on Multicultural Societies*, 5(2).

Kohli, A. (Ed.). (2001). *The Success of India's Democracy.* Cambridge University Press.

Mahajan, G. (2005). Indian Exceptionalism or Indian Model: Negotiating Cultural Diversity and Minority Rights in a Democratic Nation-State. In W. K. He (Ed.), *Multiculturalism in Asia* (pp. 288-313). New York: Oxford University Press Inc.

Mahajan, G. (2006). Negotiating Cultural Diversity and Minority Rights in India. In T.D. Judith Large, Democracy, Conflict and Human Security, Volume 2: Further Reading International Idea.

Nehru, J. (1986). *Letters to Chief Ministers.* New Delhi: Oxford University Press.

Parekh, B. C. (2000). *Rethinking Multiculturalism: Cultural Diversity and Political Theory.* Michigan: Harvard University Press.

3

Decentralization and the Strengthening of the State

A Case Study of Province of Bihar

Abinash Kumar

Introduction

The idea of decentralization is at core of any political systems which is geographically large in size, populous and democratic in nature. Democratic Republic of India is one such kind of political system which is large in geographical size and populous too. Keeping in view the democratic nature of Indian political system, the 73rd Constitutional Amendment has been introduced to decentralize the political system and the introduction of direct democracy at grassroots level.

After passing of approximately three decades of this amendment, village panchayats have been up to what extent able to fulfill the desired goals to establish direct democracy at local level. If we observe at micro level, the relevant questions are started to come in our minds like:

(i) From the functioning point of view, citizens of Panchayat do feel as part and parcel of the institution,

(ii) From the service point of view, the said services like primary education, provisioning of road and drainage, and primary healthcare facility at Panchayat have been dispensed or not?
(iii) The management of free and fair election has been established or not?
(iv) The role of family head in individual opinion to vote matters or not?

The study further tries to understand and answer these questions pertaining to Panchayats of Bihar in general and the Nawada district in particular. So, to study the Panchayat of province of Bihar accompanied with keeping in view the ethical aspects involved therein, the political behaviour of voters have been analysed through questions pertaining to functioning of Panchayat, process of election, services provided at Panchayat and management of election.

History of Bihar Panchayat

Since ancient times, Panchayats as multi-tasking bodies have been performing political, economic, and judicial functions whereas an institution at village level played as an instrument of socio-political and socio-economic developments, and the dictums as a judicial body have been well abided by the people, but later on with the coming of the British and imposition of centralized administrative system has eroded the status and legitimacy of Panchayats (Sarma, 2013: 413-422). The Panchayat for the village of India is of paramount importance so for the province of Bihar.

Keeping the importance of Panchayat in mind, the province of Bihar has started to work on this. This was the reason that just after independence, Bihar was the first province in the country which introduced the Panchayati Raj in 1948, and regular elections had been conducted till 1978 but later on the Panchayati Raj had been reduced to a defunct state and for that numerous factors were responsible (Bharati, 1989: 18).

Though, amendments have been made in the provisions of Panchayati Raj introduced in 1948 in line with the recommendations of Balwant Rai Mehta Committee in 1959, and the consequence of this amendment was the introduction of three-tier Panchayati Raj System, i.e. Village Panchayat at village level, Panchayat Samiti at Block level, and Zila Parishad at District level.

Since the grant of constitutional status of Panchayati Raj Institutions, the regular election has started to take place. The Panchayat of Bihar after 73rd Constitutional Amendment: The Bihar legislative assembly has passed the Bihar Panchayat Act to implement the provisions of 73rd Constitutional Amendment Act in province of Bihar. The provisions under 73rd Constitutional Amendment Act provides reservation of seats for marginalized sections of society like SCs, STs, and women; not less than 1/3rd (the reserved seats for women of SCs and STs included) of the total number of seats reserved for women and these reserved seats may be allotted in rotation in different constituencies thereon. But, under the Bihar Panchayat Act, the reserved seats for women are 50 per cent of total seats accompanied with the provision of up to the extent of 20 per cent reservation of seats for Extremely Backward Classes.

To understand the present condition of village Panchayat of Bihar, a micro-survey has been conducted in different village Panchayats of Bihar and primary data has been collected from 60 respondents online and offline mode accompanied with personal visits to observe the villages where questions and observation have been based on political literacy, political process, few basic services like government primary healthcare, government primary school, road and drainage condition, voting behaviour, and political culture.

The first and the most important question for any democratic political system is voting process, so is for the ongoing Bihar Panchayat Election 2021 where EVMs have been introduced for the first time for four posts and ballot paper for two remaining posts. To cast vote on EVM is not new for voters but there has been an ambiguity among the voters due to availability of both EVMs and ballot boxes at polling booths and number of symbols of different

Table 3.1: Questions asked to the People about Process of Gram Panchayat Election

Sl. No.	Questions	Responses
1.	For how many posts, EVMs (Electronic Voting Machines) are being used in Bihar Panchayat Election, 2021	Approx. 51 per cent 'Do not know', 34 per cent replied correctly and 15 per cent incorrectly
2	For how many posts, Bihar Panchayat Election, 2021 have been conducted	Approx. 69 per cent replied 'Do not know'
3	Before voting your bio-metric verification has been done if election is over in your Panchayat	Approx. 22 per cent voters have been verified, approx. 15 per cent do not know, approx. 17 per cent has not been verified and approx. 46 per cent responders said election yet to be held.

candidates on four EVMs and two ballot papers unlike Vidhan Sabha and Lok Sabha elections where symbols have been based on party line which used to be known among majority of voters. Though, to remember number of symbols for voters in Panchayat election was issues earlier but during this election, keeping ballot papers and EVMs together have aggravated the problem of voters.

In survey, it has been found that approximately 34 per cent literate responders and voters knew that for how many posts EVMs have been used and 69 per cent responders do not that how many posts there in Panchayat election. It is quite obvious that either they have not been interested in Panchayat election or knowing about it.

So, there should be uniform tools for voting for all the six posts and state sponsored awareness campaign programme to be organized at Panchayats by the State Election Commission of Bihar pertaining to election process accompanied with encouragement of youth participation in such activities like Systematic Voters' Education and Electoral Participation programme, better known as SVEEP, is the flagship programme of the Election Commission of India for voter education.

For the first time Bio-metric verification has been introduced in Panchayats election of Bihar to stop bogus voting, but, due to lack of awareness, network and power supply issues, it has not been operational at many places and as per survey, the purpose for which it has been introduced is not successful. To make it successful, it should be incorporated with the polling party instead of separate entity or agency.

So, from the above analysis, it has been clear that in most of the Panchayats, Citizens' participation in the political process is limited to voting and lack of awareness among the Panchayats pertaining to roles and responsibilities accompanied with daily activities involved there in further aggravated the sense of apathy towards Panchayats (Aiyar, 2006: 4873). The persistence of lack of interest and unawareness in activities of Gram Sabha except voting function by the citizens have been impacting the province of Bihar at large because approx. 97 per cent area of Bihar is still rural and this is a type of "parochial political culture" (Almond and Verba: 1963).

Table 3.2: Questions Pertaining to Services Provided at Panchayat

Sl. No.	Questions	Responses
1	How is the condition of road and drainage in your Panchayat	Approx. 68 per cent replied 'Good' and approx. 32 per cent replied 'Bad'.
2	The government primary healthcare facility is available in your village	Approx. 23 per cent 'Yes', approx. 59 per cent 'No' and approx. 17 per cent in bad condition.
3	How is the condition of education facility of primary government school in your village	Approx. 36 per cent 'Good', 56 per cent 'Bad' and 8 per cent facility not available.

In survey, approx. 68 per cent voters have responded that the condition of road and drainage is good and it can further be improved if maintenance services will be provided during the period for which road and drainage have been made.

The primary health care facility provided by government at Panchayat level is very poor as only 23 per cent voters replied that there is such facility and 59 per cent replied that there is no such facility and others replied that it is in bad condition.

A common school system which provides an equitable access to quality of education to every children irrespective of their different identities like caste, creed, community, language, gender and socio-economic status where minimum infrastructure like land and building; well-furnished class rooms; drinking water and toilets; playgrounds and sports facilities; libraries, laboratories and teaching aids, easy and other requirements accompanied with trained teachers and conducive teaching and learning environment which intended for nation-building and creation of social capital for country (Dubey, 2007: 2009).

When I have personally visited to different schools of different Panchayats accompanied with responses received during micro-survey of 60 persons of different districts of Bihar what I found are as follows:

(i) In most of the primary government schools, there are school buildings for name sake but without playground, library, benches, insufficient number of classrooms and toilets in bad condition.
(ii) Kitchen for Mid-day meal is either non-functional or in very bad condition.
(iii) In most of the schools, there is no boundary wall or not even wire fences.
(iv) It seems that most of the schools have been used for conducting elections and like activities not for providing educational services.

Approx. 57 per cent voters in Panchayat election have been casting their votes based on the opinion of family head which shows a kind of "Vernacular democracy" (Wouters, 2018) in Bihar. Around 90 per cent voters give preference to candidates those are educated among the available candidates. Under PRI Act, one-third of the seats have been reserved for women and in case of Bihar, it is 50 per cent. This provision intends to bring the women at front to lead at Panchayat level and same intention has been seen among

Table 3.3: Questions Pertaining to Voting Behaviour, Reservation Pertaining to Women

Sl. No.	Questions	Responses
1.	If you are not head of the family, while voting opinion of head of family matters	Approx. 57 per cent replied 'Yes' and 43 per cent 'No'.
2.	While casting your vote, which one of the following factors is the most important for you in choosing a candidate in Panchayat election 2021.	Approx. 90 per cent 'Education', approx. 5 per cent 'Caste' and approx. 5 per cent 'Sex'.
3.	There should be reservation for women in Panchayat Election.	Approx. 75 per cent replied 'Yes' and 25 per cent 'No'.

the majority of responders on the reservation for women, i.e. 75 per cent reservation for women. So, it is good sign for inclusive democracy at least at grassroots level.

Table 3.4: Questionnaire Pertaining to Management of Bihar Panchayat Election 2021

Sl. No.	Questions	Yes (%)	No (%)
1.	There should be basic facility of food and bedding for polling party at booth level to avoid any conflict with locals and to conduct the election free and fair?	80	20
2.	There should be 50 per cent security forces from CAPF to control any conflict?	90	10
3.	Age of polling party and PCCP (Patrolling-cum-Collecting Party) and Magistrate should not be more than 55 years?	70	30
4.	As an observer, do you think that there should be proper display through banner or TV screen of internal set up and procedure of room where EVMs and Ballot Boxes are kept and casting of vote will take place so that confusion among the voters can be minimized?	80	20
5.	There should be 50 per cent women polling agents at booth level?	50	50

When it comes to management of election, it is the most important part of electoral politics of any democratic political system for the Panchayat election. If due to mismanagement of State Election Commission in general and district administration led by district election officer, i.e. DM (District Magistrate) of the district in particular, election would have not been conducted free and fair then it is mockery of democracy at large. During the ongoing Panchayat election 2021 of Bihar, responses from ten (10) patrolling magistrates as an observer have been collected questions based on management part of election in which 80 per cent responders have replied 'Yes' for provisioning of "basic food and bedding facility" and "50 per cent security forces from CAPF (Central Armed Police Force)" at booth during polling so that free and fair election can be conducted. For "Display of Procedure to Avoid the Confusion among the Voters at Booth Level", 80 per cent responders replied "Yes". So, it is the responsibilities of SEC (State Election Commission) to provision the replica of internal set up of polling room on banner or TV screen just outside the room so that voting time and unintended voting can be minimized. The safety and security of EVMs and people associated with it is of prime importance. So, those who are collecting the EVMs should be physically agile to cater the needs of sensitive situation during collection and submission of EVMs without getting any kind of injuries. For the same reason, 70 per cent responders have replied "Yes" for the question that "the age of people should not be more than 55 years".

In election, 50 per cent voters are women and it has been observed that rarely any polling booth has any woman as polling agent. 50 per cent responders agreed that there should be 50 per cent polling agents at booth level to verify and help in verifying the voters so that inclusive environment can be created.

The Panchayati Raj Institution in Nawada District

The number of Naxal-affected districts of Bihar has come down to 10 and Nawada is one of ten districts and others were Rohtas,

Kaimur, Gaya, Jamui, Lakhisarai, Aurangabad, Banka, Munger and West Champaran (Ministry of Home Affairs).

Nawada District is comprised 187 Panchayats spread across all 14 blocks of the District. The vicinity of Nawada district to state of Jharkhand made the Panchayats of this district different from Panchayats of other districts because Gobindpur, Kowakole, Rajauli, Roh, Sirdala blocks have been affected by Naxals which made these Panchayats sensitive. During the micro survey specific to Panchayats of Nawada district, following facts have been found:

(a) Majority of responders are not aware about the changes made, i.e. for how many posts EVMs are being used?
(b) Most of them have given education as preference over religion, caste and sex in casting their votes.
(c) Most of them and every woman have agreed with the ongoing reservation for women in Panchayats but their faces have been used by their male relative to exercise the substantive power.
(d) All responders have replied that the condition of government primary health facility and education at Panchayat level is bad and in many villages there is no facility of primary health and primary education.
(e) Most of them replied that the meeting of Gram Sabha has rarely been conducted and a meeting may have been called if any dispute has taken place.
(f) Roads and drainage have been made in most of the Panchayats but needs improvement and regular maintenance.
(g) Bio-metric verification has been introduced but has little success.
(h) In many Panchayats, conflicts with local villagers have been reported during the election. So, deployment of 50 per cent of CAPF along with Bihar police forces is required, though, there is a dedicated rapid action force has been formed to control such conflicts but this is mobile forces and they

> have been called when such conflicts have been reported to zonal or sector officer by the many casualties may take place.

Above all, economically poor voters have been lured by money and few services in kind during the time of election by candidates. But it does not mean that voters do not prefer the candidate who will work better for the Panchayat. Corruption at Panchayat level indicates a nexus between the representatives and block officers and sometimes it becomes compulsion for representative or BDO (Block Development Officer).

Caste and sex based reserved seats under the Panchayats have been patronized in majority of the cases. In case of women of upper caste, reserved seats have been patronized by their male relatives and for other women it depends upon their economic condition if they are economically good, then, they are patronized by their male relatives otherwise by upper caste and few backward castes like Yadav, Kurmi etc. For reserved male representatives, situation is by and large same except for economically well-off candidates because they hold the substantive authority unlike most of the women.

Conclusion

Since the grant of constitutional status of third tier of government, i.e. Panchayati Raj Institutions (PRIs) in India, the procedural decentralization has come into existence. But, the substantive powers under the 11th Schedule to the Constitution are yet to be effectively transferred to Panchayat Raj Institutions (PRIs); in our parliamentary representative democracy, power between the Union and the Provinces have been shared, in the same manner it is to be transferred to local authorities by contextualizing the definition of 'the states' under Article 12 of the Constitution (Gosawami, 2015: xiv). State or province bureaucratic machinery should be in monitoring role and devolution of power under 11th Schedule to be transferred to local bodies so that the development work in Panchayat can take place according to the need of villages decided by Gram Sabha like Vidhan Sabha not based on the directions of provincial government and much bureaucratic control because it has been seen in many cases and it seems that "Mukhiya" is not the constitutional authority as treatment meted out to them by bureaucrats. Gram Sabha is an instrument of direct democracy at local level but due to lack of Voters' education at grassroots level, voters' participation has just been limited to voting. But even after passing of three decades of its implementation, the substantive sense of democracy is by and large missing due to negligence by state government in terms of financial grant initially, persisting social structure at village levels and political illiteracy among the villagers related to functioning of Panchayat. If the proper election management, by inculcating a political culture to be an active, participatory and interested citizens to empower them and creation of conducive environment for easy access to services like basic education, primary health, road, drainage facilities at local level would be planned, executed and maintained in long run and in true sense then it can strengthen democracy at grassroots level and it will further educate and prepare the citizens for Vidhan Sabha and Lok Sabha elections in better way. The politically aware citizen based on democratic values can strengthen the institution of state.

References

Almond, Gabriel & Sidney Verba (1963). *The Civic Culture: Political Attitudes and Democracy in Five Nations*, Princeton, NJ: Princeton University Press

Aiyar, Yamini (2006). "Decentralisation and Democracy" [Review of Local "Democracy in India: Interpreting Decentralization", by Girish Kumar]. *Economic and Political Weekly*, *41*(47), 4873-75. http://www.jstor.org/stable/4418946

Bharti, Indu (1989). "Decay of Gram Panchayats in Bihar", *Economic and Political Weekly*, 24(1), 18-19. http://www.jstor.org/stable/4394212.

Dubey, Muchkund (2007), "Road Map of a Common School System in Bihar", *Economic and Political Weekly*, *42*(29), 2999-3005. http://www.jstor.org/stable/4419807

Gosawami, Sandhya (2015). *Introduction: xiv, in Troubled Diversity: The Political Process in Northeast India*, Oxford University Press: New Delhi.

Sarma, M. (2013), "Gram Sabha the Artifice of Rural Development: A Glimpse of Kamrup District, Assam". *The Indian Journal of Political Science, 74*(3), 413-22. http://www.jstor.org/stable/24701052

Wouters, J.P. (2018), *In the Shadows of Naga Insurgency: Tribes, State and Violence in Northeast India*, Oxford University Press, New Delhi.

4

Decentralization, Inclusive Development and Impact of Smart City Mission in Srinagar City of Jammu & Kashmir

Muzafer Rasool Hajam, Manvendra Singh and *Rubaya Akther*

Introduction

The theoretical framework and practical connotations of governance mechanisms and public administration witnessed transformative changes in the post-colonization era. Much of these changes can be attributed to the need for paced reforms in government priorities to facilitate socio-economic development and public welfare in newly emerged independent nations. The academic research debated the relevance of the politics-administration dichotomy approach in the new global framework in the context of varying levels of socio-economic development in developing countries. The emerging concerns of widespread poverty, hunger, illiteracy, malnutrition, healthcare, unemployment, and climate change took the central stage in the governance policies. The administrative reforms are facilitated by the incorporation of political and administrative decentralization, New Public Management (NPM), Comparative Public Administration

(CPA), Development Administration, New Public Administration (NPA), New Public Governance (NPG), and New Public Service governance approaches.

The developing countries, including India, started various flagship programmes to alleviate the widespread poverty, ensure participatory governance, and facilitate inclusive socio-economic development in the rural and urban landscape. Mahatma Gandhi National Rural Employment Guarantee Act, Sarva Shiksha Abhiyan (SSA), Samagra Shiksha Abhiyan, National Education Policy-2020, Atal Mission for Rejuvenation and Urban Transformation (AMRUT), and Smart City Mission are some of these national flagship administrative interventions to transform India into global economic and knowledge hub, through cooperative federalism and competitive federalism collaborations with regional governments including the Union Territory of Jammu & Kashmir.

Decentralization

Due to the increase in state functions, diversification of public welfare programmes, and ensuring effective coordination, monitoring, and control of multiple public agencies, the governments across the globe adopted political and administrative decentralization by empowering local self-government institutions and administrative delegation. The emphasis towards decentralization processes has been more visible in developing nations, including India, due to the emerging concerns of marginalization, poverty and the need for sectoral development policies like agriculture, education, commerce and trade, healthcare and other basic rural and urban services, viz. housing, food security, electricity, drinking water, public transportation, waste management, drainage services, and digitization.

The decentralization frameworks in India are facilitated by constitutional empowerment of local democratic institutions through 73rd and 74th Constitutional Amendment Acts, ensuring community-based socio-economic development and participatory democracy. The reforms in Indian bureaucracy have facilitated integration and collaboration of public administrative setups by removing hierarchical structures and promoting horizontal communication networks between public agencies. The establishment of the National Institution for Transformation of India (NITI Aayog) paving the way for a bottom-up approach in public policy planning is another step towards decentralization and inclusive development due to its emphasis on community participation in the development process and formation of development plans in the context of diversified regional needs and aspirations.

However, of late, the concept of decentralization is being critically analyzed because of mushrooming of public agencies and emerging concerns for timely monitoring and supervision by the institutional chief executives, which has led to a reshuffling in governance paradigms and adoption of the re-centralization policy by merging allied administrative institutions and rationalization of staff in concerned departments, to ensure effective performance outcomes and timely institutional coordination.

Inclusive Development

Inclusive development refers to holistic and equitable socio-economic planning mechanisms involving a participatory development approach to protect all citizens' fundamental rights and political and administrative empowerment of marginalized sections in the population through affirmative actions. The United Nations led the global agenda to mitigate emerging concerns in the 21st-century world by emphasizing reforms in governance institutions and public policies to alleviate widespread poverty, food insecurity, housing, illiteracy, healthcare, and personal safety, and environmental pollution and climate change. The frameworks of Millennium Development Goals (MDGs) and Sustainable Development Goals (SDGs) are pivotal global efforts towards inclusive development emphasizing administrative re-orientation and governance reforms in the member countries to ensure fulfillment of set targets as enunciated under the MDGs and SDGs mechanisms.

The recent global data about the prevalence of socio-economic and political inequalities reflect the inadequacy and ineffective implementation of inclusive development policies. Despite unprecedented technological progress in the 21st century, the growing wedge between 'haves' and 'have nots' is alarming. According to the OXFAM International-2020 report, the world's 2,153 billionaires' wealth is more than the collective wealth of 4.6 billion people, i.e. 60 per cent of the world population. While the wealthiest 10 per cent of adults in the world own 85 per cent of global wealth, the bottom half of the world population own only 1 per cent of global wealth. As per the World Bank 2020-report, while the global illiteracy level among the population of 15 years and above age still stands at 13 per cent, illiteracy among females is higher (16%) than that of males (10%). As per the UN-WOMEN 2021-report regarding women's political participation, 119 countries have never had a women leader, only 21 per cent of ministerial posts are held by women globally and only 25 per cent of all national parliamentarians are women. All these reports regarding this uneven world mandate proactive policy interventions and allied research studies to realize objectives of participatory governance and inclusive development as enunciated under the United Nations' Sustainable Development Goals (SDGs) Programme.

The need for inclusive development is felt more in third-world countries like India. A large section of the population is still marginalized and deprived of socio-economic benefits because of various historical, cultural, and socio-political reasons.

Literature Review

Decentralization, inclusive development, and participatory governance have been debated over the years by academicians, researchers, and administrative practitioners across the globe, more so due to increasing socio-economic inequalities in the 21st century.

Caroline Paunov (2013), using an analytical framework for evaluation of different types of income inequalities, evaluated different in-depth perspectives of inclusive development, role and impact of technological advancement and innovations on leveraging economic inequalities, particularly among lower-income groups. The study findings suggest innovations in business mechanisms and technologies impact income inequalities through income distribution, and the innovations in social and business are vital for diminishing socio-economic inequalities and ensuring inclusive development.

Glyn Williams (2004) analyzed the intricate relationship between participatory development and political control by exploring the multi-faceted interdependence of socio-economic development and the politicization of administrative institutions. The author emphasizes that empowerment must be an open-end ongoing engagement process wherein participation strengthens and stabilizes politics.

B. Christens & P.W. Speer (2006) comprehensively studied theoretical and practical connotations of participatory development, its pros and cons and its relevance in terms of interdisciplinary transformation with concepts such as empowerment, urban planning, psychology, and civic engagement. The study suggests a pragmatic approach towards the study and practice of participatory development coherently and systematically.

Andrea Cornwall (2000) empirically analyzed prevalent participatory development practices in Asia and Africa regarding gender equality and women empowerment to reveal a skewed and lopsided approach in inclusive planning and development policy. The study suggests a varied interpretation of gender roles and diminished involvement of women in the development process apart from emphasizing rethinking of gender and issues of powerlessness to ensure equitable and inclusive development.

Brahmanandam & T.B. Babu (2016) traced the educational development of STs in India, analyzing causes for their educational backwardness and socio-economic marginalization. The authors relate high dropouts and educational marginalization of tribal communities to their distinct lifestyle, being geographically and socially isolated, and suboptimal policy to ensure culturally linked education. The study advocates concerted efforts and inclusive policy interventions for the socio-economic and educational development of the tribal community.

To ensure inclusive development and promote participatory governance in Jammu & Kashmir, concerted efforts and integrated policy approaches are needed to realize these affirmative programmes' objectives and ensure socio-economic upliftment and political empowerment of marginalized groups, paving the transition towards inclusive and participatory development in the region. Prevailing political conflict in the region has led to increased poverty and affected development initiatives by creating impediments in implementing development policies (D.A. Mahapatra *et al.*, 2008). Multiculturalism and plurality of the political landscape are the hallmarks of Jammu & Kashmir due to distinct geographical regions diversified by multiple factors, viz. ethnicity, religion, region, and caste they were facilitating demands for the creation of local autonomous development authorities (A.A. Wani, 2013). Loss of public faith in governance, suspicion towards political establishments, rampant corruption, alienation of masses from the national mainstream, and political instability are fundamental impediments in the region's development (N. Kumar, 2010).

Objectives of the Study

(i) To explore decentralization and inclusive development mechanisms in the Srinagar city of Jammu & Kashmir.

(ii) To analyze the impact of the Smart City Mission on inclusive development in the Srinagar city of Jammu & Kashmir.

(iii) To evaluate administrative interventions for rejuvenation of inclusive development and participatory governance in Jammu & Kashmir.

Research Methodology

The study used both primary and secondary data sources. The study is based on analysis and interpretation of data collected through a public survey in Srinagar—the capital city of Jammu & Kashmir, using simple random sampling and questionnaire method, and 50 research respondents from different age groups, socio-economic status, gender, and education levels. Also, significant secondary data sources, including research publications, articles, government reports, books, and websites, were consulted to evaluate various facets of decentralization and inclusive development mechanisms, emphasizing analyzing participatory governance reforms in Jammu & Kashmir.

Results and Findings

The study's results and findings explored after comprehensive analysis and interpretation of the primary data collected from the general public comprising fifty respondents from the Srinagar city of Jammu & Kashmir and secondary data sources are discussed below.

Impact of Srinagar Smart City Mission on Decentralization, Inclusive Development and Delivery of Public Services

The Srinagar Smart City Mission approved in 2017 enunciates key infrastructural projects like roads, open spaces and other public utilities, public health institutions, waste management and sanitation, and social forestry for environment protection, citizen grievance redressal cells, as well as a host of other smart projects aimed at improving service deliveries to facilitate inclusive development in the capital city of Jammu & Kashmir. For this purpose, a Special Purpose Vehicle 'Srinagar Smart City Limited' has been set up administered by District Development Commissioner as Chief Executive Officer of the said authority.

However, Srinagar city has witnessed skewed planning policies with sluggish implementation and a futuristic planning approach. The city is ranked at 49th position among 111 cities in Union

Government's 'Ease of Living Index' for 2020, at the bottom last 49th position under Smart City Mission rankings, 2021 and received 16th slot under AMRUT mission rankings-2021. Poor air quality, insufficient water availability, waste management and energy demands are the burning demands of an urban environment in Srinagar city.

The issues of basic civic amenities like housing, drinking water, electricity, roads, open spaces, waste management, drainage, communication networks, and internet facilities were highlighted during interaction with the research respondents through questionnaires to analyze the availability and quality of these public services along with the evaluation of public satisfaction about these services. The level of citizens' satisfaction with the services was measured on a 1-5 Likert scale. The results reveal that the majority of the citizens are either unsatisfied or least satisfied about public services delivery in the Srinagar City of Jammu & Kashmir, while only 18 per cent of the respondents are fully satisfied with drinking water services, only 8 per cent show satisfaction with electricity services. Similarly, the data also reflects lesser public satisfaction about waste management services (only 2% fully satisfied) and drainage services in the Srinagar city (only 10% fully satisfied).

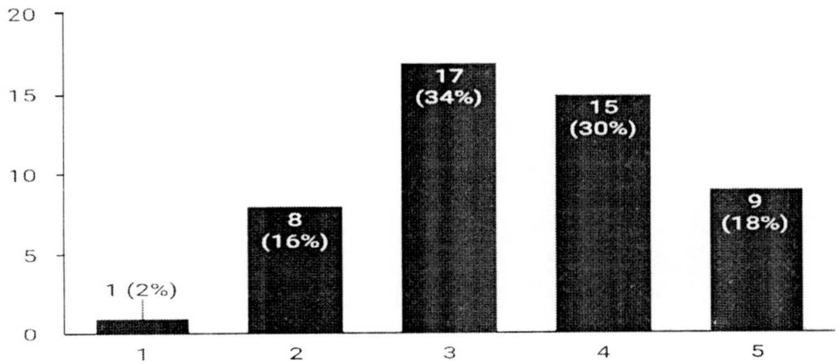

Fig. 4.1: Public satisfaction about drinking water service

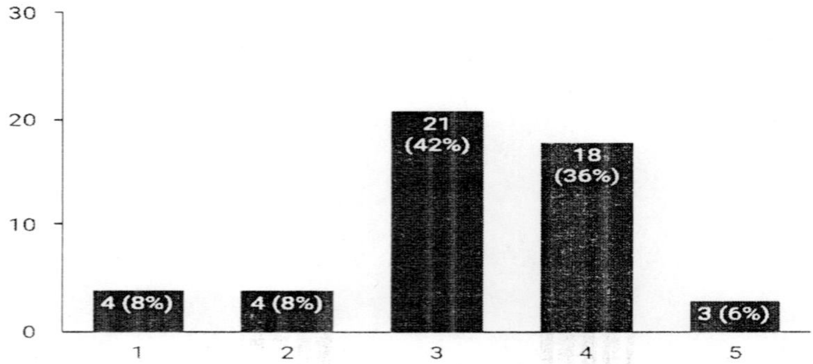

Fig. 4.2: Public satisfaction about electricity service

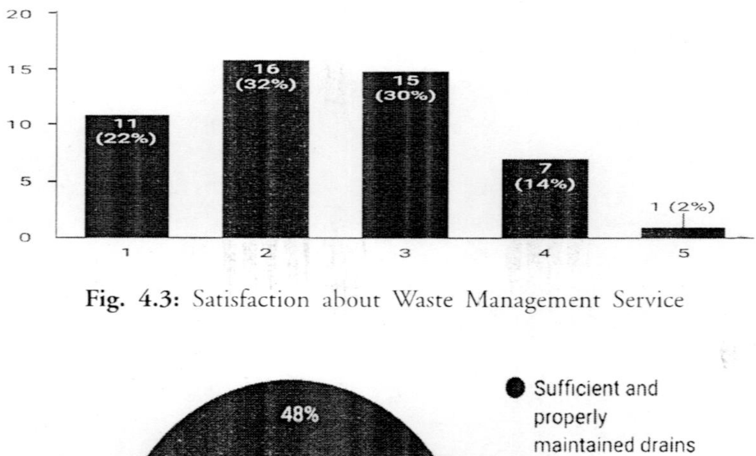

Fig. 4.3: Satisfaction about Waste Management Service

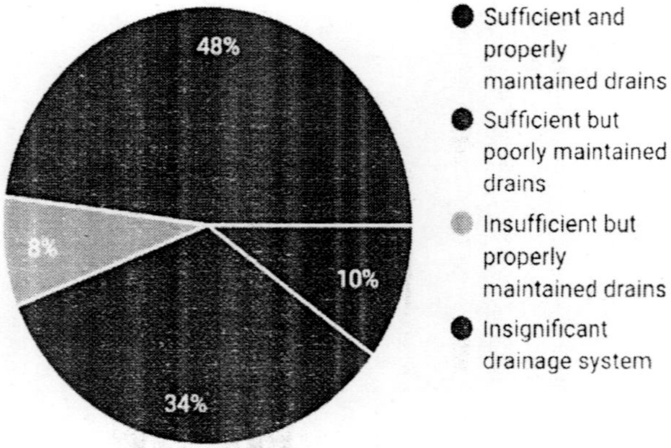

Fig. 4.4: Public satisfaction about drainage services

Also, the level of public satisfaction about transport services and online government services as provided in the Srinagar city, is very less, as only 2 per cent of the respondents show satisfaction about transport services, while as only 14 per cent of the respondents are fully satisfied with the online government services provided in the Srinagar city of Jammu & Kashmir.

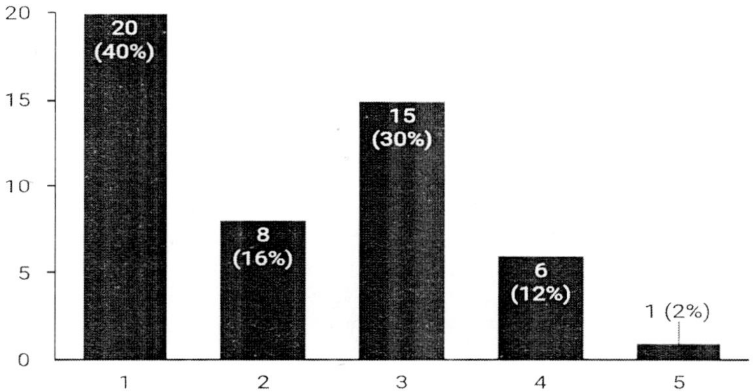

Fig. 4.5: Public satisfaction with transport services

The analysis of the data received from research respondents reflects various governance challenges in the Srinagar city, with 'corruption' being rated as the biggest administrative challenge followed by 'lack of coordination' among government agencies as another major hurdle in the governance of the city.

Administrative Interventions by Jammu & Kashmir Government to Rejuvenate Inclusive Development and Participatory Governance

To improve inclusive development paradigms and to ensure participatory governance the Jammu & Kashmir administration implemented the following governance measures.

Fast Track Recruitment in Public Services: To address the staff shortage in public offices and rising unemployment levels in the region, the administration has started a fasttrack recruitment policy for the speedy advertisement of all pending vacancies in the public offices and time-bound completion of the selection process through regional recruitment agencies.

Increased Fund Allocation for the welfare Programs: J&K administration has facilitated pooling of financial resources by integrating various welfare schemes like Widow Pension Scheme, Integrated Child Development Scheme, Elderly Pension Scheme and increased financial support for inclusive inclusion development programmes through facilitation from the Central Government.

Introduction of Geo-Spatial Tracking (GST) and Management Information System (MIS) Technologies in Public Offices: The innovative and smart technologies are being introduced in public office to facilitate 'e-office networks' for real-time file tracking and performance monitoring and to avoid administrative delay and red-tapism.

BEAMS and E-Tendering

BEAMS: Department of Finance has started a smart financial transaction application, Government of Jammu & Kashmir, to facilitate smooth payment gateways among government offices and online tendering government projects have been started through the E-Tendering process.

Performance Review and Compulsory Retirement of Public Servants: J&K administration recently amended civil services conduct rules to mandate periodic performance review of public servants and compulsory termination of the underperforming or corrupt government employees in all public office.

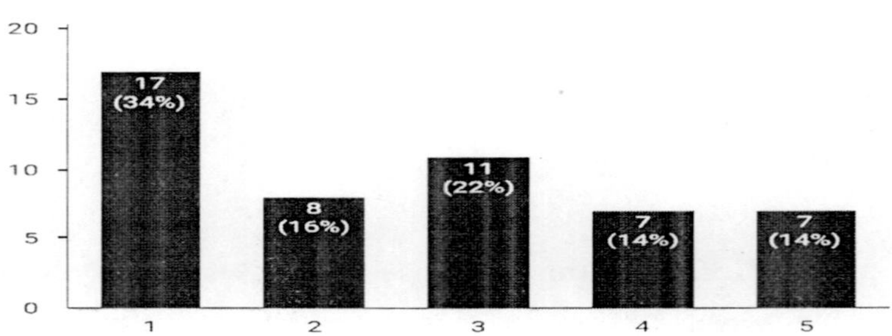

Fig. 4.6: Public satisfaction about online government services

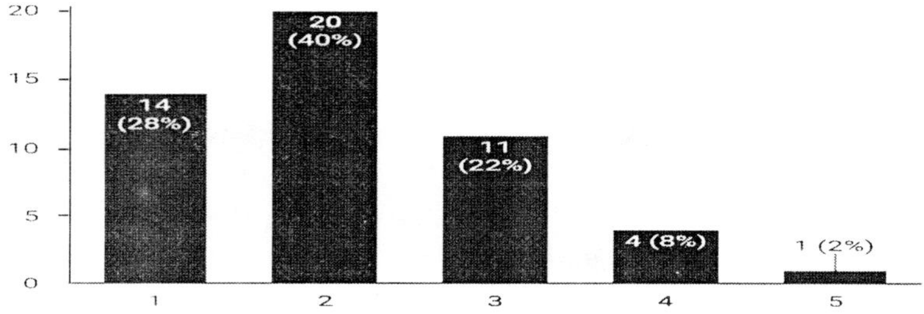

Fig. 4.7: Public satisfaction about the overall development of Srinagar City of J&K

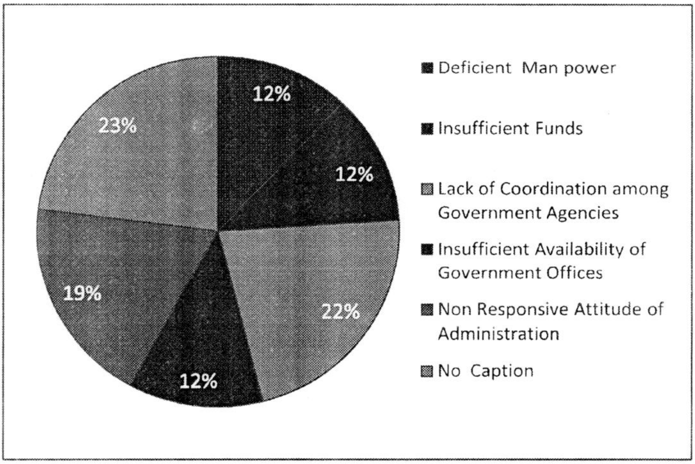

Fig. 4.8: Governance challenges in the Srinagar city of Jammu & Kashmir

Conclusion

The governance and public policy paradigms are witnessing dynamic transformation due to decentralized delivery of public services and emphasizing participatory governance and inclusive development to mitigate prevalent socio-economic inequalities and alleviate emerging concerns of global poverty, illiteracy and other basic civic amenities in the rural and urban landscape. The United Nations emphasize re-orientation of the prevalent bureaucratic mechanisms, particularly in developing countries like India, to ensure responsive and accountable public administration systems. The Indian government's flagship urban development programme, Smart City Mission, ensures participatory governance and inclusive development in regional cities, including the Srinagar city of Jammu & Kashmir. The Srinagar Smart City Mission is yet to realize the goals of inclusive development and the mission objectives due to staff deficiency in the implementing agencies and lack of institutional coordination. Rejuvenating governance institutions through capacity building and policy evaluation is needed to promote good governance and ensure participatory development.

References

https://ww.oxfam.org/en/press-releases/worlds-billionaires-have-more-wealth-46-billion-people

https://data.worldbank.org/indicator/SE.ADT.LITR.ZS

https://www.unwomen.org/en/what-we-do/leadership-and-political-participation/facts-and-figures

Caroline Paunov (2013). Innovation and Inclusive Development: A Discussion ofThe Main Policy Issues. *STI Working Paper*. (1). pp. 1-63.

Glyn Williams (2004). "Evaluating Participatory Development: Tyranny, Power and (Re)Politicization". *Third World Quarterly*. 25(3). pp. 557-78.

B. Christens & P.W. Speer (2006). "Tyranny/Transformation: Power and Paradox in Participatory Development". *Qualitative Social Research Forum*. 7(2). pp. 1-10.

Andrea Cornwell (2000). Making a Difference? Gender and Participatory Development. Institute of Development Studies Discussion Paper - 378. pp. 1-39.

Brahmanandam & T.B. Babu (2016). Educational Status among the Scheduled Tribes: Issues and Challenges. *The NEHU Journal*. XIV (2). pp. 69-85.

D. A. Mahapatra *et al.* (2008). The Peace Process and Prospects for Economic Reconstruction in Kashmir. *Peace & Conflict Review*, *3*(1). pp. 1-17.

A. Wani. (2013). "Ethnic Identities and the Dynamics of Regional and Sub-Regional Assertions in Jammu & Kashmir". *Asian Ethnicity*. 14(3). pp. 309-41

N. Kumar. (2010). "Jammu and Kashmir: The Emerging Contours and the Way Ahead". *Manekshaw Paper*. Centre for Land Welfare Studies, New Delhi. pp. 1-28.

5

The Dynamism of Decentralization from the Perspective of 'Suppleness' of the Strong States

A Theoretical Study

Rukmini Bhattacharjee

The decade of 80s of the 20th century witnessed a remarkable upsurge of interest in the State and its institutions. The comparative-historical studies examined the formation of national states, the disintegration and rebuilding of states in social revolutions, the impact of states on class formation, ethnic relations, women's rights, and varied modes of social protest. Economic historians and political economists have theorized about states as institutions of property rights and the role of the States as regulator of the market. The cultural anthropologists have explored the special meanings, purposes, and activities of State in the non-Western settings. The renewed interest in the study of the State and specifically with respect to the market may be considered as a part of the process of "political development", which is itself an evolutionary concept. It, however, ended up being more relevant in the context of international and domestic struggles over state building than the rationale for socio-economic "differentiation" in the context of nation-states. The autonomy of the States is largely conceived as organizations which claim control over territory, resources and population and are reflective of the demands or interests of social groups, classes, or society at large. It is re-enforced through an assessment of the capacities of the State to implement envisioned goals despite actual or potential opposition of powerful social groups and/or recalcitrant socio-economic circumstances. The "strengths" or "weaknesses" of States as sites of more or less independent and effective execution of official actions constitute an integral aspect of the legitimacy of State action.[1] States are traditionally identified with centralized structure of government for being considered as strong and resilient. Strong States are usually identified with unitary rather than federal government which have a marked concentration of power in the executive branch. States with centralized policy formulation structures and processes are often capable of independently working towards specific goals without significant obstruction. The identification of centralized States as strong States is based on their capacity to exercise greater control over the inhabiting population, attaining conformity in the legal procedures thereby facilitating the concentration of authority at the higher levels of the chain of command, these thereby ensure legitimization of centralized government's structure and functioning.[2]

The years leading to the decade of 1990s witnessed an incremental but significant democratic transition across different nations of the world. This transformative changes in governments are related in the literature of democracy as the "Third Wave". Samuel Huntington is his epochal work *The Third Wave: Democratization in the Late Twentieth Century* (1991) elaborated the causal factors which may be held responsible for the origin of the Wave. Huntington identifies several factors of which the most impactful was the withering away of legitimacy of authoritarian regimes due to increased popular expectation of regular, free and fair elections as potential safeguards against militarization of governmental functional. This was closely followed by the modernization of the less developed economies coupled with the economic crisis during the 70s of those regimes which used economic growth for their legitimization. However, the modernization of the economies released structural changes like increased rates of urbanization, education and a rising middle class which constituted a constellation of social forces with the organizational capacity and awareness to demand democratic governance. Besides, the international actors pressurized for the respect of human rights and the powerful States were marked as hindrance to the sustenance of the Third Wave which transpired from the 1970s through to the 1990s. In the view of Huntington, there was a "demonstration effect" which contributed to the broadening of the Third wave of democracy.[3]

These transitions in democracies overlapped with the emerging consensus on decentralization. The proponents argued that decentralized structures of governance are likely to be more effective in strengthening the State. Decentralization came to be interpreted as not an alternative to centralization rather as an integral part of a continuum. Thus, they need to be practiced as complementary principles because both are essential to strengthening of the States. The complementarity of the national and sub-national actors should be determined by an analysis of the most effective methods and ways of achieving a relevant objective.[4]

The distribution of authority and responsibility from the Central Government to subnational or quasi-independent governments or agencies or the private sector organizations for the execution of public functions is usually interpreted as decentralization. Decentralization can take different forms—political, administrative, fiscal and market—these differ with respect to their characteristics, policy implications and conditions for successful and efficient functioning. There can be different versions and combinations of decentralization across countries, within countries and even within sectors. Thus, what is more feasible is a dissection of the approach of decentralization rather than any established definition of decentralization from the perspective of the strong States.[5]

Decentralization as a working idea may be conceived as the assignment of powers of the national government to regional or local authorities with definite objective. If centralization is in response to the need for the national cohesion, decentralization is a response to the demands for diversity. By 1980s a consensus was taking shape that neither too much centralization nor absolute local autonomy or a combination are not desirable. Moreover, it can be detrimental from the perspective of an efficient system of collaborative effort of the national, regional and local centres of decision making and implementation. However, the renewal of interest in decentralization is shaped by the recognition that less centralized decision-making tends to be more effective by the way of making local governments and civil society more proficient in the execution of their own responsibilities. A closer study of decentralization reflects three major trends relating to its practice:

- **Deconcentration:** It is a limited form of decentralization which involves the continuous appearing of new distribution of responsibilities among the constituent units of the government, i.e. national, regional and local levels of government.
- **Devolution:** It reflects a new form of decentralization with the disengagement of the State and economic liberalization.
- The expanded involvement of local jurisdictions and civil society in the management of their affairs with new forms of participation, consultation and partnerships.

Decentralization by devolution is defined by the transfer of functions, resources and decision-making to citizens themselves, who would exercise the powers ceded to their local government or their representative organizations. The new reforms through this process of decentralization are characterized by four major changes which tend to increase the goal of complementarity of effective administration and local democracy:

- New forms of subnational jurisdictions may be created at the regional or local levels;
- The extension of universal suffrage to include all subnational jurisdictions;
- Provisions need to be established for allocation of sufficient financial resources to subnational governments; and
- The elimination of the *a priori* supervisory role of state representatives, and the institution of legal administrative control (administrative tribunals), and a *posteriori* control of budgets.

Thus, decentralization by devolution is motivated by the need to respond to regional demands, which reflect the awareness of a community of interests at the sub-national level and the aspirations of the citizens to participate in the management of their affairs. It is likely to result in the strengthening of institutions, and the coordination and conformity of actions with the objective of efficient administration.[6] Decentralization is a process of bringing the government "closer to the people" which enforces the ground-up processes in state-building. The literature on State strength widely referred to various aspects which make States strong. According to Fukuyama (2004) two dimensions of the States determine their capacity—state strength *versus* state scope. The hallmark of "stateness" in his view is determined by the enforcement functions of the states rather than the scope of its activities. This brings into discussion the impact of decentralization on the strength of the State. This leads to understanding of decentralization as a reform which supports or expands the exercise of political power of subnational units *via* the devolution of power and resources to the locally elected officials at the subnational units. Such arrangements improve state assets and responsibility for service delivery to the people at the grassroots level. It is rooted in associating the capability of the states to exercise authority over a defined territory and its population. Thus, decentralized institutions in federal arrangement have been recommended as an arrangement to "hold together" the fractured multi-national states. It assumes that decentralization promotes the formation of multiple but complementary identities that enable the citizens to simultaneously carry both ethnic identity as well as identify with the polity as a whole. The opponents of decentralization claim devolving power and resources at the subnational level will support secessionist aspirations of citizens who believe local authorities are more able to provide services and manage public budgets efficiently. However, the proponents claim that the devolution of power and resources to even secessionist politicians with vested interests are likely to generate opposite response by the way of increasing their responsibility and commitment. Federal arrangements are successful in both developed and developing nation-states with strong regional identities but also strengthen national identities such as the United States, Germany, India and Brazil. These federal democracies validate the proposition that decentralized government can stitch together diverse identities and at the same time act as a protective shield to eliminate the tendencies of sub-national tyranny or secession.[7]

It is argued that decentralization through proper design can deepen democracy without compromising on State strength. It is ideally an accepted notion that a well-designed decentralization can foster higher levels of participation and legitimacy which lowers the cost of maintaining order, compels respect for the law and reduces the need to show power. The ability to mobilize resources and provide services with the view to maintain opposition at a lower level and keep transaction costs modest as that would bolster the legitimacy of the democratic practices that underpin these desired outcomes. Decentralization increases social learning which produces a dynamic that strengthens the State from the grassroots upward. Decentralizing a State strengthens its democratic strength by involving engagement of stakeholders at the grassroots level. The "suppleness" of the State is assured by strength of democratic processes. The increase in the density of government structures and most importantly participation, representation and engagement of the people generate feedback chains which enhance the overall level of answerability of the government. This serves to improve state's sensitivity to local aspirations and complaints. This also seeks to correct the issues which tend to result from overlapping of responsibility and multiple redundancies in the policy realm. The suppleness of the State reflects the strength of the State which largely implies the stability and capacity of the government. It loudly speaks about the health of the State, i.e. absence of malaises which tend to disintegrate or fail the States. An estimate of the suppleness of the States may be made from the strength of the State which is the ability to assert authority over a territory and its inhabitants. Decentralization enables this by promoting local cultural and ethnic identities by the process of dispersing authority from the national to sub-national centres. It is decentralization which enhances the presence of the States by ensuring that the interests of citizens across the country are emulated in policy and public services. The representation of the regional and local interests and identities at the national level through the legislation and policies play the role of ironing out fissiparous tendencies in the constituent units. This aptly avoids the likelihood of local governments becoming "little tyrannies", by accommodating their demands in the discourse of national politics. So, the design of decentralization is of critical importance in enforcing local-accountability mechanism which makes the citizens responsible for their decision and actions. The power-sharing among the constituent units through the channel of decentralization is effective in determining the suppleness of State capacity. Decentralization for instance may play an effective role in the avoidance of fiscal imbalances. The suppleness of the States is reflected in the absence of hindrances to the implementation of policies at the regional and sub-regional levels. By contrast, the inability to implement the goals is indicative of the subversion of policy objectives by government agents and clearly stands for a weak State. Such weak States are embodiment of internal disturbances and rifts. The proponents of decentralization claim the involvement of many representatives in the decision-making process which typically stands for greater stability of the policies, thereby supplements the strength of the State.

The suppleness of the State is drawn from the coordination and cooperation rather than command and control. This consequent resilience constrains the failing of the national governments. The dynamism of decentralization increases the state strength by magnifying democracy institutionally. Strong States consider the delivery of public services as one of its primary functions because quality service delivery often tends to make governments legitimate and authoritative and that too through the means of popular consensus. Such activities and their outcomes enable the States to grow strong and supple. The delivery of public services in a decentralized arrangement boosts greater governmental accountability. Of all the ways, social learning may be considered to be the most powerful tool through which decentralization makes States strong. Decentralization enriches social capital by social learning because it ensures learning by doing. It articulates the shared preferences and aggregates shared preferences and thereby enforces accountability.

A critical scrutiny of decentralization may indicate that it is often not the ideal means to ensure equitable allocation of resources and instead more risks may arise from overspending. However, overspending might trigger fiscal imbalances and macroeconomic problems which eventually is harmful for stability and strength of the State. Decentralizing taxation and spending, prohibiting bailouts and setting hard budgets will be useful in mitigating these risks. It is not the fault of decentralization *per se* but its poor design which hinders the actualization of its positive impact and can thus be remedied by improving rules and sub-national incentive structure. Moreover, the decentralized systems enable the co-production of goods and services for social welfare at all the levels of administration, i.e. national, regional and local levels which extends the capacity of the States and thereby amplifies their suppleness. The most impactful effect of decentralization on State's strength is determined by the structure of government. Its effect on the democratic norms and practices further the suppleness of the States. Decentralization affects democracies by the means of encouraging participation which results into transparency and legitimacy of the States and eventually its suppleness. The promise of decentralization deepens democratic suppleness in States which thereby sustain stronger States and better governance.[8]

Notes

1. Skocpol_Bringingthestatebackin_Summary.pdf
2. state_WP_2014.pdf
3. TheThird Wave: DemocratizationintheLateTwentiethCentury-Wikipedia
4. Decentralization.PDF (undp.org)
5. BriefingNotes_decentralization_WB.pdf
6. AHistoryofDecentralization(ciesin.org)
7. Faguet_Fox_Poeschl_Does-decentralization-strengthen-or-weaken-the-state_WP_2014.pdf
8. lse.ac.uk_storage_LIBRARY_Secondary_libfile_shared_repository_Content_Faguet,J-P_Decentralizing_deeper_democracy_Faguet_Decentralizingdeeper democracy_2015.pdf

6

Decentralization and the Supple State

An Indian Experience

Meena Rani

Introduction

One of the major questions confronting developing countries is which political-administrative system can work best to combat their pressing problems like poverty, corruption, and inefficiency—centralization or decentralization? Public administration academics and practitioners have often viewed this problem with the lens of the nature of the state. The idea of a strong state favours centralization. On the other hand, democratic concerns go with decentralization. In the 1990s, the idea of a strong state as a centralized state became less favourable as decentralization came to be preferred all over the world due to sweeping democratic reforms. In recent years, as the conflict between different local groups arises in many countries, the need for a 'supple state' has been felt. The recent threats such as pandemic, poverty, regional and religious conflicts demand the process of decentralization and a 'democratic suppleness' of the state.

Decentralization

Defining decentralization is no easy task. This is because this term is used in a variety of contexts, related to different meanings and applied in different ways. A set of thinkers refers the term for federalism and autonomous units in a federal system. Others explain decentralization as a transfer of power from a central government to local self-governing institution. Before understanding the concept of decentralization, it is necessary to differentiate it from other ways to transfer power away from the centre. Decentralization is generally regarded as de-concentration, delegation, privatization, and devolution. Decentralization is defined as a reform that establishes or increases the critical power of sub-national units *via* the devolution of power and resources to locally elected sub-national officials. This is different from administrative de-concentration where Central Government delegates some of its functions to local agents but retains overall decision-making control. This is different from delegation, where managerial responsibility is transferred to organizations outside the regular bureaucratic structure and from privatization, where state assets and responsibility for service delivery are transferred to the private sector. Decentralization is also described in three forms—political, administrative, and fiscal. Generally speaking, administrative and fiscal decentralization comes after political decentralization. Political decentralization can be understood as a system in which local units at the grassroots level have autonomy and powers of decision-making and self-governance. In administrative decentralization, decentralization refers to the transfer of power from centre to local governments. In general terms, decentralization is directly related to localness. Decentralization saves localness in this globalized era. According to the World Bank, decentralization can best be understood as a political process in the sense of the devolution of resources, tasks, and decision-making power to democratically elected lower-level authorities, which are largely or wholly independent of Central Government (World Bank, 2000). Though there cannot be an acceptable definition of decentralization. A section defines it as a sharing of power.

Decentralization and India: A Brief History

Why are some countries more decentralized than others? Experts have attributed such differences to cultural, political, institutional, and geographic factors. India has a colonial legacy that has affected the level of democracy and economic development in the country. When India got independence in 1947, it inherited a strong unitary structure of government. After independence, it was felt that decentralization could not be permitted beyond a certain point due to the risk of political and other forms of instability. Later a significant initiative was taken by Prime Minister Rajiv Gandhi and P.V. Narasimha Rao governments that eventually led to granting constitutional status to the Panchayati Raj Institutions. Through the 73rd and 74th Constitutional Amendments, apart IX-A was added to the Constitution. These Amendments give a substantial shift in the process of decentralization of India. The Act signified in clear terms the intention of the state to strengthen the process of third-tier federalism in India.

Decentralization in India: Present Status

We can understand the phenomena of decentralization in India through three different aspects—political, administrative, and fiscal. Political decentralization visualizes greater participation of people in the decision-making process. It also aims to give more power to the elected representatives so that they can have more influence in the policy-making and implementation at the grassroots level. Political decentralization depends on constitutional reforms that strengthen the political autonomy of local units. The 73rd Constitutional Amendment in 1992 is an example of political decentralization. Administrative decentralization contains the set of policies that redistribute authority and responsibility for the delivery of social services from the central government to local authorities. Fiscal autonomy is a key element of decentralization.

It has been seen that fiscal decentralization empowers regional governments to raise sufficient revenue from local sources, and this reduces their dependence on the national government. On the other hand, the lack of fiscal power to local governments reduces the prospect of revenue mobilization at the local level. Therefore, it is very important to have a sufficient amount of revenue for the local unit to effectively carry out the work assigned to them. Fiscal decentralization comprises the set of policies that aim to increase the revenues of local units. "An increase of transfers from the central government, the creation of new sub-National taxes and delegation of tax authority that was previously National are all examples of fiscal decentralization." One observer rightly points out that "73rd Amendment strengthens administrative federalism in order to facilitate and encourage delegation of administrative and financial powers from the state to the local bodies. It would be proper to assess the significance of democratic decentralization in India by analyzing the level of progress made by the initiative. Using the conventional classification of political, administrative, and fiscal decentralization the World Bank's three-volume study of Indian decentralization ranks India among the best performer internationally in terms of political decentralization but close to the last in terms of administrative decentralization."

India as a Supple State

Suppleness could be defined as flexibility and it is assessed by seeing how easily a system can sustain and adapt itself amidst rapid environmental changes. Lose of suppleness means an inability to adjust and respond in changing complex situations. Thus, a supple state is attributed with decentralization, autonomy, resilience, and robustness. Though, the concept of suppleness is fundamentally different from robustness and resilience as sustainability of a system is often characterized by either robustness or resilience. According to Hiroki Sayama, "Suppleness is about the sustainability of a real biological or ecological system. Although those systems definitely can be robust and resilient, their states never remain at a single place in a long term. Instead, they continue to change dynamically due to complex interaction and evolutionary adaptation of system components. What is sustained over a long period of time in those systems is not a specific normal state, but the ability to demonstrate a unique dynamic meta-state such as alive, active, productive and so on. Some of those meta-states may be readily quantifiable and measurable, while others are more qualitative and may be hard to quantify. By shifting focus from the system's specific state to its dynamic meta-state, one may consider yet another characterization of sustainability which I call suppleness." Therefore, suppleness is a by-product of decentralization. In other words, a supple state must be a decentralized one. "Just as the flexibility of an aircraft's wings increases the aircraft's resilience through their capacity to dissipate shocks, we argue that decentralizing a state may increase its strength by making it more supple.

India is characterized by more ethnic and religious groups than most other countries of the world. Aside from the much noted two thousand caste groups, there are more than six major religions, many languages spoken in various dialects in 28 states and 8 union territories and is substantial number of tribes and sects. Due to this multi-ethnic and multi-religious character of Indian republic, caste-religious conflict has become a continuous factor rather than an occasional one. When we come to discuss the means to resolve these challenges and difficulties, decentralization is widely endorsed as a solution. Decentralization gives an empowering voice to the local citizens by bringing the government closer to the peoples. Panchayati Raj in India can be seen as a best example of this. Now people living in rural areas can more easily raise concerns with public authorities and find a local solution to their local problems. Thus decentralization goes with more participation and reach of the people. But the critics argue that by dispersing power from the centre to local units, decentralization tends to deepen and widen the gap between different ethnic and religious groups, which weaken the efforts towards national unity. Although this is not completely wrong, the question arises as to how decentralization be designed that holds fractious group together rather than promotes secession? The answer lies in decentralizing power and authority to a level below that of ethnic, linguistic or other identity groups. In this way empowered sub-national units would tend not to be identified with group identity or privileges. Rather than stoking divisive tensions, local governments will instead become identified with issues of efficiency and service provision. Along with this, by giving territorially concentrated groups the power to make their own decisions about issues that most interest them, decentralization can also accommodate diversity and protect groups against abuse or neglect from the centre or from one another.

In India, each state has strong regional identities like Marwadi in Rajasthan, Marathas in Maharashtra, Punjabis in Punjab, Tamils in Tamil Nadu, Malayali in Kerala etc. Decentralization plays a major role to protect these identities and prevent to make them fractious as it can accommodate diversities and protect groups against the suppression of the centre. In this way, decentralization improves the elasticity of the government and makes them supple. Another major argument against decentralization is about strong state. Generally, it is perceived that strong state is essentially associated with centralization. This is, however, not as simple as decentralization *versus* strong state debate. Advocates of decentralization argue that more minds in the policy-making actually make them more stable.

Decentralization cannot be seen as a simple choice between strong central unit and weak local unit of government. It would be far more prudent to view it "as a move from a strong centralized command structure that is simpler and cleaner but ultimately more brittle in the sense of susceptible to failure in any of its parts, to a system that is more complex, based on more actors with independent sources of overlapping authority, where coordination and cooperation are far more important than command and control for the system as a whole to operate well. This greater complexity is more difficult to manage, and coordination harder to achieve than command adherence. But it also implies greater suppleness.

During the COVID-19 pandemic, decentralization and peoples' participation has played a key role in crisis management across the world. India is no exception to this general trend. During the first Coronavirus wave, Kerala model, Bhilwara model, the Dharavi model became success stories due to decentralized approach. On the other hand, the second wave which is characterized by centralized Covid task forces and war rooms were not effective in delivering real time rapid responses. We can, therefore, say that poorly planned decentralization may create the problem but these problems can be solved by decentralizing the activities with low economies and delegate taxation. And effective response to a pandemic also depends not only on national characteristics and healthcare system but also on a country's political and administrative decentralization.

References

A. Bagchi and Tapas Sen (1989). *Fiscal Decentralisation in India*, National Institute of Public Finance and Policy, New Delhi, March.

Hiroki Sayama (2010). "Sustainability of social systems by Suppleness", *SSRN Electronic Journal*, October.

Jean-Paul Faguet, Ashley M. Fox and Caroline Poschl (2014). "Does decentralization strengthen or weaken the state? Authority and social learning in a supple state? Is decentralization good for development?, Oxford University Press.

Jean-Paul Fauget, Ashley M. Fox and Caroline Poschl (2015). "Decentralizing for a deeper democracy and a more supple state," *Journal of Democracy*, August.

Kiran Mazumdar-Shaw (2021). "A decentralised approach could help turn the tide against Covid," *The Mint*, May 10.

M. Govind Rao (2015). "For a true decentralization," *The Hindu*, November 2.

Prabhat Kumar Dutta and Inderjeet Singh Sodhi (2021). "The rise of the Panchayati Raj Institutions as the third tier in Indian federalism: where the shoe pinches," *Indian Journal of Public Administration*, April.

Tulia G. Falleti and Kellogg Institute (2004). "Theory of Decentralization and its effects on the intergovernmental balance of power: Latin American cases in comparative perspective," Kellogg Institute, July.

Younis Ahmad Sheikh (2014). "Democratic Decentralisation in India: An Overview," *International Journal of Social Science & Interdisciplinary Research*, July.

7

Decentralization through Local Self-Governance in Pulwama, Jammu & Kashmir

Tavseef Ahmad Mir and *Manvendra Singh*

Introduction

Decentralization is the dominant trend in matters of governance all over the world. Various forms of decentralization are practised in developed and underdeveloped countries of Latin America, Africa, and Asia. Decentralization has been considered as a significant procedural as well as the institutional framework for the phenomenal industrial growth as well as for increasing the efficiency of the governance in the last two decades in China, but in India, the process started in a slow manner which reached to its climax after 73rd Constitutional Amendment. The reforms of 1990 changed the paradigm of governance altogether. The centralized state lost its relevance, and more decentralization became the order of the day. Decentralization provided a wide range of benefits to the overall governmental structure. The ideals of the welfare state enshrined in the Constitution could be fulfilled by taking this procedure.

It is argued that the decentralization process reduces the role of a state, but it creates checks and balances at every government level, enhancing responsiveness, transparency. With the introduction of technological and scientific developments, it becomes imperative to have mini or smaller areas or markets which could be managed more efficiently. To maintain equilibrium and stability, it is also the primary tool to have peace and lesser conflicts. It is because of more tremendous advantages that this process has received much importance all over the world. Different countries have moved ahead with it in different formats. This process involves three sub-processes which are political, executive, or administrative, and fiscal. Devolution of Administrative powers pertains to the physical structure and working of the local levels of government, whereas political decentralization deals with the way politically appointed heads to various levels of local government. The fiscal aspect considers the budgetary and expenditure procedures among the local levels of governance and the Central Union Government. From an economic perspective, decentralization helps the lower levels of government effectively decide the points of service deliverance that could be administered effectively. It creates competition among various government agencies, which enhances the public's choice of the service provider at par with the taxes paid. Authority or power given to the elected leaders at lower levels of government falls within the sphere of political decentralization. It gives the public the power to make decisions, which reflects the local interests. It gives representation to multicultural or social perspectives in governance. Instead of a homogenous national policy, political decentralization makes the local aspirations more reflective of diverse sections of the society. It empowers the masses to question various government policies and programmes, which increases the quality of governance. Political decentralization forms the backbone of the whole decentralization process as it is intimately connected with the public.

Panchayats are considered as institutions of self-governance in the 73rd Constitutional Amendment. There is a fixed five-year term for Panchayati Raj Institutions (PRIs), which are elected through universal adult franchise. It has empowered these institutions to deliver essential services like health, sanitation, primary education, and supervision of other welfare schemes. It has been left to the state governments to decide which powers would be decentralized to these institutions. There are variances among various states regarding this aspect. Some states have evolved more powers, and some have lesser. This amendment has mandatory provisions for all states to create a three-tier local governance system at the grassroots level Village, Intermediate level Block and Apex District levels. It has provided legal status to all the three tiers of Institutions. Moreover, the amendment deals with four main issues: the constitution of panchayats, their powers and authority, their elections, and their relationship with other departments. This Constitutional Amendment has not enabled PRIs only politically, but it has made the states duty-bound to create a conducive situation for Panchayats in operational, financial matters of administration. At the international level, decentralization has generated many positive outcomes like enhancing efficiency and reducing corrupt practices. Representatives who live among the people can effectively specify their needs, which would lead to more effective and efficient public services. There is a sustained cycle of providing better services and better collection of taxes, which increases the economic strength of the institutions to provide high-quality services. This chapter tries to define the decentralization concept through different aspects, measures taken to revive Local Self-Governance and the linkage between decentralization and perceptions of empowerment among the masses in District Pulwama of Jammu & Kashmir. We selected one hundred participants from the district, and they were contacted through different modes of communication, and a questionnaire was provided to them.

Local Self-Governance in J&K

In Jammu & Kashmir, elections for constituting local self-governance institutions were connected with the special status of the erstwhile state. As the provisions of the 73rd Amendment were not applied, it was usually up to the whims and fancies of the ruling party when to conduct an election that only for the panchayat level. The intermediate Block Development Councils were never constituted. Elected persons at the district level did not head District Boards, but the government selected heads. There were no concrete measures to empower these institutions. In total, the culture of local self-governance was absent. After 5th August, 2019, when the Central Government annulled special constitutional provisions and the erstwhile state was designated as a Union territory, the Union Government initiated various measures to give a new life to these governance structures. Panchayat elections were conducted. Later, the elected personnel from these panchayats elected chairpersons for block development councils. In the year 2020, direct elections were held for constituting District Development Council. A District Development Council (DDC) is the apex body at the hierarchy of elected local government institutions under the Jammu & Kashmir Panchayati Raj Act and its appended Rules. These Councils consist of representatives from both rural and urban areas for planning sustained development in the district. Every district has fourteen DDC Members, who elect a chairperson and vice-chairperson among themselves. The Deputy Commissioner of the district is the secretary of the Board. Representatives from urban bodies are also part of this body. District Development Councils replaced District Planning and Development Boards (DDB), which were functional in the erstwhile state of Jammu and Kashmir. DDC formulates yearly plans for the overall development of the district and supervises the functioning of lower-level LSG institutions. Election Authority in the form of State Election Commissioner was appointed. These initiatives resulted in the full implementation of the mandate under the 73rd Constitution Amendment. Another important measure was the Back to Village Programme. This also resulted in the taking of governance to the doorsteps of the people. Through this programme, various higher-ranking bureaucrats personally visited the countryside and discussed the necessities fulfilled by approving the necessary budgets.

Local Self-Governance in Pulwama

Pulwama falls within the Kashmir valley of Jammu & Kashmir Union Territory. This district has geographical as well as political importance in the Union Territory. As per the 2011 Census, this district is inhabited by an approximate population of 5.60 lakh and 1090 square kilometres, divided into 8 Tehsils comprising 327 villages for administrative convenience. The district is located on the southern side of the valley of Kashmir. The district's economy is mainly agriculture-dependent as it is famous for Rice production and quality Saffron, which is renowned all over the world. The district leads milk production in the whole Union Territory, called "Anand of Kashmir".

Pulwama has fourteen DDC Constituencies: Achgooze, Aripal, Awantipora I, Awantipora II, Dadsara, Kakapora-I, Kakapora-II Litter, Newa, Pampore, Pulwama I, Pulwama II, Shadimarg, Tral and nine-Block Development Councils are Achgooze, Aripal, Awantipora, Dadsara, Kakapora, Litter, Lasipora, Pampore, Pulwama and Tral. There are five Municipal Committees in the district.

Results and Discussions

We received responses from the participants, which are discussed as follows:

1. *Access to Government Developmental and Welfare Schemes through Local Self-Governance (LSG) Institutions*

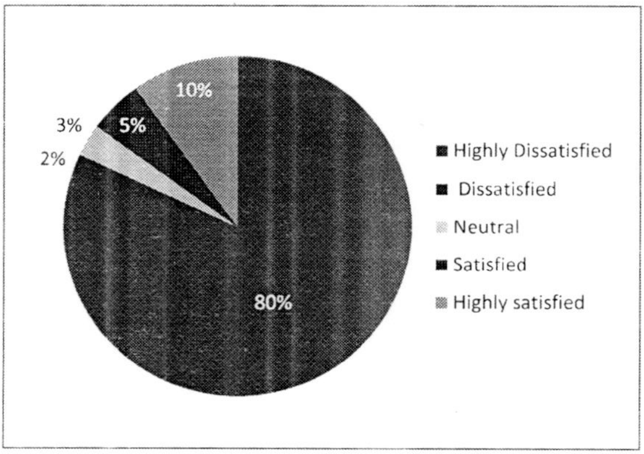

Fig. 7.1: Accessibility

Regarding this issue, 8 per cent were highly satisfied, 10 per cent were satisfied, 5 per cent neutral, 3 per cent dissatisfied, and 2 per cent highly dissatisfied. The results of this question are illustrated in Fig. 7.1. These results show that the empowerment of LSG institutions has made access to government developmental and welfare schemes easier.

2. *Transparency in Local Governance Increased after the Local Self-Government Elections*

About this issue, 74 per cent of participants were highly satisfied, 6 per cent were satisfied 2 per cent neutral, 10 per cent were dissatisfied, and 8 per cent were highly dissatisfied. The results are illustrated in Fig. 7.2. These results portray a perception among masses that these governance measures are transparent and there are fewer chances of dubious activities.

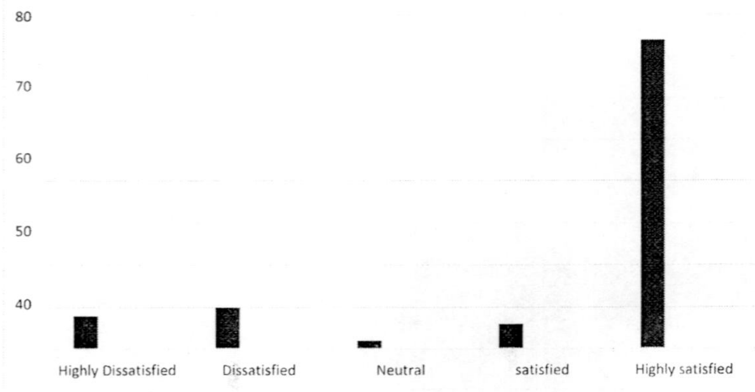

Fig. 7.2: Transparency in Governance

3. *Perception of Corrupt Practices have Decreased at Grassroots Levels of Government*

79 per cent were highly satisfied with this issue, 1 per cent were satisfied, 5 per cent neutral, 10 per cent dissatisfied, and 5 per cent

highly dissatisfied. The results are illustrated in Table 7.1. People find that corrupt practices have diminished to a great extent. It is because of greater transparency and mass participation. Another factor is that of empowerment of Anti-Corruption agencies.

Table 7.1

Highly Dissatisfied	Dissatisfied	Neutral	satisfied	Highly satisfied
5	10	5	1	79

4. *Participative Governance has Increased through Local Self-Government Measures*

87 per cent of participants were highly satisfied that LSG measures have increased public participation in governance. 4 per cent were satisfied, 1 per cent neutral, 3 per cent dissatisfied, and 5 per cent highly dissatisfied. The results are illustrated in Fig. 7.3. Plans are formulated for the *Halqas* at *Halqa* meetings, where all the elders of the locality discuss and formulate developmental plans as per the requirements. This measure has given a feel to the masses of having a share in local governance issues.

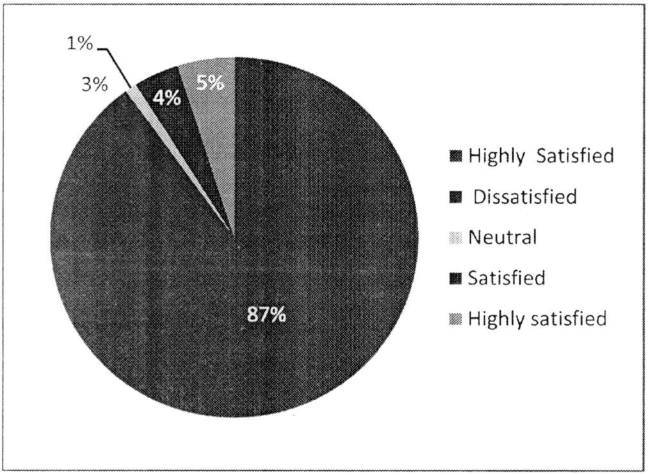

Fig. 7.3

5. *Behaviour of Elected Representatives of LSG towards the Public*

62 per cent of participants were highly satisfied, 3 per cent were satisfied, 11 per cent neutral, 12 per cent dissatisfied, and 13% highly dissatisfied. The results are illustrated in Fig. 7.4. Concerning this issue, there may be various factors affecting it. Due to peculiar political and security situations, there was less participation of the public in Panchayat elections. It resulted in the winning of less popular representatives. However, for DDC Elections, there was comparatively better participation. It may be emphasized that these newly taken measures would take time to settle down entirely in the overall governance paradigm. Over time, these institutions will get more strengthened, and the public participation would increase, resulting in the election of more competent representatives.

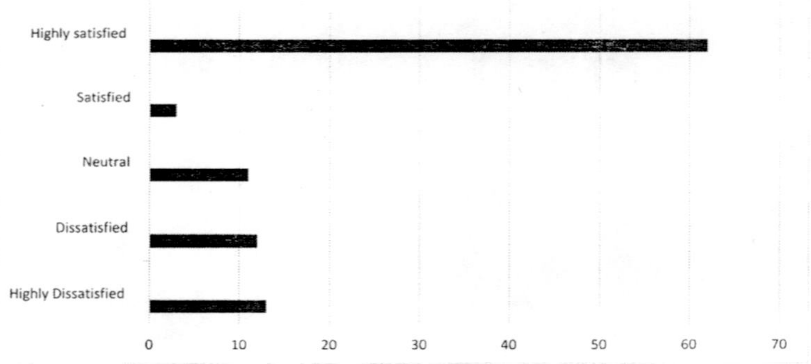

Fig. 7.4: Behaviour of elected Representatives

Conclusion

The initiatives regarding reviving and empowering the Local Self-Government Institutions by the Union Government and the Union Territory administration have strengthened local self-governance institutions. A new chapter of participative governance has been started in this region. There is a more robust perception among masses of belonging to these structures of governance. Quality of governance has increased, and the masses feel that these initiatives have led to an increase in participative governance, transparency which has further led to a decrease in incidences of corrupt practices. Timely disbursement of funds to these Institutions would necessarily strengthen them and make them more effective. The government needs to strengthen these institutions further, resulting in good governance in the Pulwama district is unique and the whole Union Territory in general.

References

Bardhan, P. (2002). "Decentralization of Governance and Development". *Journal of Economic Perspectives*, *16*(4), 185-205. https://doi.org/10.1257/089533002320951037

Dick-Sagoe, C. (2020). "Decentralization for Improving the Provision of Public Services in Developing Countries: A Critical Review". *Cogent Economics & Finance*, *8*(1), 1804036. https://doi.org/10.1080/23322039.2020.1804036

Inakhiya, G.K. & Sharma, M. (2016). "Decentralization and Panchayati Raj Institutions in Jammu and Kashmir: An Overview". *Public Affairs and Governance*, 4(2), 145. https://doi.org/10.5958/2321-2136.2016.00012.6

Mookherjee, D. (2015). "Political Decentralization". *Annual Review of Economics*, *7*(1), 231-49. https://doi.org/10.1146/annurev-economics-080614-115527

Purfield, C. (2004). "The Decentralization Dilemma in India". *IMF Working Papers*, *4*(32), 1. https://doi.org/10.5089/9781451845143.001

"Riabokon, V. (2020). "Decentralization is the Way to Rural Development in Ukraine". *Ekonomika APK*, *1*, 6-17. https://doi.org/10.32317/2221-1055.202001006

Sharma, B. & Kaur, J. (2018). "Community Development and Panchayati Raj in India. *Journal of Advances and Scholarly Researches in Allied Education*, *15*(4), 1-5. https://doi.org/10.29070/15/57102

Tyagi, D.R.C. & Siddiqui, T.S. (2017). "Functional and Financial Devolution to Panchayati Raj Institutions in India: A Study of Uttar Pradesh". *International Journal of Scientific Research and Management*, 5(7). https://doi.org/10.18535/ijsrm/v5i7.39

Vengroff, R. & Salem, H.B. (1992). "Assessing the Impact of Decentralization on Governance: A Comparative Methodological Approach and Application to Tunisia. *Public Administration and Development, 12*(5), 473-92. https://doi.org/10.1002/pad.4230120505

8

Challenges to Decentralization and Tribal Development

A Study of State of Himachal Pradesh

Abhishek Sarta

Introduction

There is no exact definition or the parameter for defining a tribe. However, researchers have defined it differently from time to time. At times they define "Tribe" as "aboriginal" or "depressed classes" or "Adivasis". Generally, a "tribe" can be defined as "a group of individuals during a primitive or barbarous stage of development acknowledging the authority of a chief and typically regarding them as having a same ancestor."

Gillin and Gillin says "Tribe is any collection of pre-literate local group that occupies a common general territory, speaks a common language and practices a common culture". In the Indian Context, T.B Naik has illustrated some characteristics features of a tribe as follows:

- A tribe should have very limited functional inter-dependence within the community, is economically backward.
- Its population lives in an isolated geographical area.
- Having a common language.
- Politically unorganized and community panchayat are quite influential.

- Have their own customs and norms.

The Scheduled Tribe population in the state is mainly concentrated in the three districts of the state, namely Kinnaur, Lahaul and Spiti and some parts of Chamba district. The tribal population in the state is nearly 6 per cent of the total population. According to the Census 2011 the population of Himachal Pradesh is 68,64,602 of which 3,92,126 (5.71%) belongs to Scheduled Tribes. However, the people belonging to these tribes live in the terrain where life is challenging (Lahaul, Spiti, Kinnaur and Chamba districts) and their access to public services is very limited, which gets reflected in the poor health and education infrastructure in tribal areas as well as low levels of human development. The official list of Scheduled Tribe population in Himachal Pradesh includes tribes like Gaddis, Gujjars, Kinnara, Lahaulas, and Pangwalas. There are some other small tribes which includes Bhot, Beda, Khampa, and Swangla. The ST population is quite dominant in Lahul & Spiti and Kinnaur—two rural districts of the state, where they contribute to 81 per cent and 58 per cent of the total population of the districts respectively.

Name of District	No. of Census Villages (Inhabited)	Total Population	Scheduled Tribe Population
Bilaspur	953	381956	10693
Chamba	1110	519080	135500
Hamirpur	1671	454564768	3044
Kangra	3617	1510075	84564
Kinnaur	241	84121	48746
Kullu	314	437903	16822
Lahaul-Spiti	280	31564	25707
Mandi	2850	999777	12787
Shimla	2705	814010	8755
Sirmour	968	529855	11262
Solan	2383	580320	25645
Una	790	521173	8601
Total	**17882**	**6864602**	**392126**

Source: Himachal Pradesh Census 2011.

Constitutional Safeguards for Scheduled Tribe Population

The Constitution of India provides for some constitutional provisions for the protection and development ofTribal population of the country. Promoting educational and economic interests and providing the people belonging to these areas protection from injustice and any forms of exploitation. The Constitution also empowers the States to make reservation for tribal people in public services in case of inadequate representation in the services. The Constitution says there should be a separate department in the States and National Commission at the Central level to promote tribal welfare and safeguard their rights and interests. The states are provided grant-in-aid to meet the cost of any such development schemes to be undertaken for prompting the welfare of Scheduled Tribes or improving the level of development in the Scheduled Areas, Article 275(1).

The constitutional safeguards for protection and development of the tribal are:

- Article 14 talks about equal rights and opportunities for everyone;
- Article 15, prohibits discrimination on grounds of sex, religion, race, caste etc.;
- Article 15(4), says that the state should make special provisions for the STs;
- Article 16(3), empowers states to make reservation in appointments for STs;
- Article 46, states to promote with special care educational and economic interests of STs, protection from social injustice and exploitation;
- Article 275(I), grant-in-aid for promoting the welfare of STs;
- Article 330, 332, 335, related to the reservation of seats for STs in Lok Sabha and State Assemblies; and
- Article 339, 340, related to Control of the Union over the Welfare of STs and powers to investigations thereof.

- One of the important Acts which ensures Social Safeguards of the STs is "Scheduled Castes and the Scheduled Tribes (Prevention of Atrocities) Act, 1989."

These provisions create an environment of affirmative action, which helps in supporting the ST population and makes them a part of the mainstream. All these measures enable the tribal population to be at par with the other social communities. These protections give the tribal a platform for their growth and development and also makes them a part of the system.

Fifth Schedule Areas

Under the provisions of 'Fifth Schedule' of the Constitution of India, there are areas which require special protections and administrative measures to implement policies related to development of the area. Kinnaur and Lahaul-Spiti districts and Pangi and Bharmour areas of the Sub-Divisions of Chamba district is considered as the Scheduled Areas in the State, as these areas fulfill the minimum eligibility criteria of 50 per cent ST population concentration in a Block. So these three districts are put under the Fifth Schedule in the state of Himachal Pradesh.

HP Panchayat Raj Act, 1994

This Act mandates the constitution of Panchayati Raj in the state of Himachal Pradesh with a three-tier system for local governance and Democratic Decentralization. The Act also provides for representation to women and people belonging to tribal communities in all the three-tiers in accordance with their population proportion. Panchayat extension to Scheduled Areas (PESA) did not extend to the state till 1997. It was through the Second Amendment in the H.P. Panchayati Raj Act, 1997 the provisions of PESA became functional in the state. The focus of the Act was to protect the customs, rights and livelihoods patterns of the tribal communities with special focus on participative and people-centric governance, planning and policy implementation.

The PESA Act ensured that there is effective participation of tribal people in the decision-making process they have a say what can work better for them and what kind of development they want for their areas based upon needs.

Objectives of the Study

The main objectives of the study are as follows:

- To highlight the challenges which are there when it comes to decentralization and development of tribal areas.
- To study the issues and problems related to socio-economic development of these areas.
- To study the pattern of budget allocation for tribal welfare and the development of tribal areas by the government.
- To study various programmes and policies by the Government of Himachal Pradesh for the development of the tribal areas.

Methodology

The study highlights the challenges of decentralization that are faced by the people and the government when it comes to the implementation and execution of the policies and programmes meant for the tribal population, tribal area development. The study is based on the secondary data. The data for the study is collected from the secondary sources, like journals, magazines, books, reports of the Himachal Pradesh government or the sponsoring agencies related to tribal development programmes in the state and the different official websites of Himachal Pradesh Government and government of India.

Decentralization simply means involving the community at large or involving the people in the decision-making process. As in case of decentralization in tribal area it has to do with the functioning of local government at the grassroots level of democracy and how people are involved in the development prospect at the very basic level of democracy that is the Local government or the panchayats (PRIs). The practice of decentralization is concerned with how far the policies framed by the State or the Centre Government for the development of these areas are implemented on the groundlevel with the help, involvement and of the locally elected representatives in the PRIs and the general public.

Challenges to Decentralisation in the Tribal Areas of Himachal Pradesh

Decentralization as a concept sounds quite engaging and gives an impression of participative management but it is a complex process which involves coming together of people, pooling of ideas, arriving at a consensus and so many other things. The development of any area largely depends upon how involved the people of that area in the process of decision making. Similarly, in case of tribal areas this holds true and penetration of government policies and programmes depends heavily on the participation of local community. But there are many problems in institutionalising the process of decentralization in the tribal areas also. Some of these challenges are as follows:

Awareness among the Tribals: There is a lack of awareness among people in the tribal areas regarding their rights, duties, initiatives of the government, different programmes and policies of the government. The people are not in a position to decide what is good and bad for them. Lower level of literacy also have a bigger role to play in creating this information deficit.

Geographical Location of These Areas: These tribal areas are located in the far-off places from the city. These areas are not accessible in all seasons because of the weather conditions and difficult terrain. Therefore, it becomes a difficult task to involve the local people in the development and it is difficult for the people living here to show their participation in every work at the local level as it involves visiting of different government offices and officials from time to time to get their works done.

Accountability Issues: It is because institutions like Gram Sabha is not working efficiently what otherwise would have been the social audit of the development works undertaken in the particular tribal area does not happen because there is a lack of awareness among people and people do not feel that these local government institutions are doing any better in their lives. So, because of this the phenomena of Social audit hardly occurs in these tribal areas and the representative are not held responsible for spending of grants on related to the development works, progress of development works and the overall functioning PRIs at the local level

Financial Constraints: The states have a financial dependence on the Centre for majority of its developmental programmes. Similarly, in case of PRIs, the resources with the state are not adequate to carry out developmental works which hampers the development of these tribal areas. And at the same time money raised by these institutions (PRIs) through taxations and collection of fees is very minimal which hardly makes any difference.

Participation of Local Community: The participation of people in the development of their area is comparatively very low in the tribal settings. To ensure accountability and development of the area, people hardly show their presence in the meetings of Gram Sabha. The people are more into their own work and hardly show any interest in taking part in the decision-making process and the development of the local area.

Problem of Inclusion: Inclusion simply means that giving equal opportunity to every section of population. Here, in this case inclusion means giving people belonging to different caste, age, gender a chance to represent these local bodies (PRIs), to make decision as it brings a different erective and different societal problems get highlighted. But this inclusion is limited as only a few influential people controls the local bodies. The most disadvantageous are the women as they are to some extent confined to their homes in these rural settings and keep themselves away from all these operations. However, provisions of reservation are there but the spirit behind this is still overpowered by factors like money, influence, lack of awareness.

Issues Related to Socio-economic Development of Tribals in the State of Himachal Pradesh: There are social and economic problems concerning the people who live in the tribal areas which somehow makes them a disadvantageous group and creates a gap when it comes to needs explanation here to substantiate this para because of this information deficit neither they take want to participate on their own development and overall progress of these areas in comparison to other areas and local bodies (PRIs). Some of these issues are highlighted below:

Education: Access to education is relatively low in the tribal areas and there is not much of a choice when it comes to schools, colleges, institutions of higher education in the tribal areas. The students from these areas migrate to cities like Shimla, Dharamshala, Chandigarh for their studies. In the year 2011, the overall literacy in the state was nearly 83 per cent. Whereas this literacy percentage among Scheduled Tribes is 73.64 per cent which is almost 10 per cent less than the state's average, at the same time female's literacy rate stood at 64.20 per cent which makes it further worse. The avenues for higher studies are also very less in these tribal areas.

Health Services: The remoteness of tribal areas, also creates barriers in terms of health services available for the people of the area. The hospitals are very few in number and they are far from place as the population in these areas are scattered. On top of that technology, specialisations are limited making it even more difficult. There is not much to offer when it comes to health facilities, the people have to come to the cities in order to avail the health facilities.

Road Connectivity: The connectivity of the far-off places to the main cities and the places having basic amenities is not proper. There are places where roads are poor and in winters or rainy seasons the connectivity of that places get cut-off. This is because of the difficult topography which creates this geographical divide in the tribal, It restricts the access to basic goods and services, markets and creates a very high dependency among the tribal population on natural resources for their basic livelihood. Majority of the roads in these areas are not black coated which makes their condition worst during rains and winters.

Infrastructure Needs: Tribal areas are situated in far off locations from the main cities, access to these geographical locations is difficult, extreme weather condition makes these area a difficult place to live with lack of basic facilities. This isolation leads to the problems of communication, residential, educational and medical facilities. Communication also includes transportation related facilities. These undeveloped means of transportation also hurdles when it comes to linking the areas with any development plan/ scheme, building supportive infrastructure and projects.

Problem Related to Storage and Marketing: There is a problem of storage for surplus agricultural or the horticulture produce in these tribal areas. The lack of storage creates a condition of wastage of produce and financial losses to the agriculturist in the area. At the same time, there are limited sales and marketing opportunities available with the producers which further makes it difficult for the producer to gain benefits out of their produce.

Very few Employment Opportunities: The employment opportunities in the tribal areas are very less as there is not much of industries or the corporates so only few public sector jobs are available which are also through open competition making it limited for the residing population. So, the majority of tribal population is dependent on agriculture for their livelihood needs, and this agriculture is also rainfed which makes it dependent on weather and rainfall pattern.

Therefore, as a result many of the people from these areas migrate to the cities in order to get their livelihood needs fulfilled.

Grazing Issues: As the tribals have a nomadic way of living they have livestock and for the rearing of these animals they are dependent on the forest for grazing. But in the recent times there has been a substantial increase in the flock size of transhumant resulting in grazing issues for the livestock of these tribal people. And at the same time forest land is being used by the government for various other activities causing a reduction in the grazing land for the livestock. The tribal are time and again appealing the government that the grazing land should only be used for animal rearing and should be only kept for the use of tribal community.

Spending pattern (Budgetary Allocation) of the Government for Protection, Growth and Development of Tribal Areas and Tribal People in the State of Himachal Pradesh:

How much money the government puts in some development work or for the welfare, upliftment of the people does play a very important role in shaping up the desired outcome. The spending pattern from the government's side on tribal welfare and development have been on a high in the recent past, continuous efforts are being made by the government to secure these people social justice and equity. Working on its commitment towards equitable and balanced development of the tribal areas and welfare of tribal people of Himachal Pradesh, the state government has ensured that it has the adequate allocation of funds for the development of tribal areas and people residing in these areas.

Programme	Year	Budget Amount
Tribal Area Development Programme	2018-19	567Cr
	2019-20	639Cr
	2020-21	711Cr
	2021-22	849Cr
Border Area Development Scheme	2018-19	25.95Cr
	2019-20	27.50Cr
	2021-22	25Cr

Inferences from the Table

- The spending by the government for development in the tribal areas increased over the years.
- Increased spending simply means that more developmental works are being undertaken by the government in these areas and these areas are not neglected when it comes to budgetary allocations and development schemes.

Steps Taken by the Government of Himachal Pradesh for the Development of Tribal Areas and Various Policy Implications

The Scheduled Tribes and Other Traditional Forest Dwellers (Recognition of Forest Rights) Act, 2006: This Act says that the rights to use the forests rests with the community of Scheduled Tribes who have been living in these areas for generations now. The Act empowers the tribal living within designated areas to use the forest resources in a sustainable way with efforts towards conservation as well. It gives them the right to use and dispose of minor forest produce. It also gives them the right to habitat, access to biodiversity, water bodies, grazing right, and so on.

The Scheduled Castes and Scheduled Tribes (Prevention of Atrocities) Rules, 1995: This Act provides certain protection to the people belonging to Scheduled Tribes and power to State Governments to frame rules for the same. This Act protects these people against atrocities and any form of exploitation being caused of them by anyone. Further under the Fifth and Sixth Schedules it gives special powers to the States for Protection and Governance of these people and to frame rules for reservation to give them equal representation in the legislatures and the public sector jobs.

Tribal Sub-Plan: The purpose of having a tribal sub-plan was to have separate programmes, policies, and focus for the tribes and the tribal areas. Such a plan is a part of the overall plan of a state and is, therefore, called a sub-plan. Under the tribal sub-plans, additional benefits are given to the tribal people. It is in addition to the things which are promised under the general overall plan. Therefore, it is a way of ensuring social equity in addition to equality.

Tribal Development Department: This Department came into existence in the year 1976 with the main objective and focus of the social and economic upliftment of the Scheduled Tribes. The idea is to promote the interests and welfare of the Scheduled Tribes and work in close knit with the other departments and the ministries to ensure the development of these tribal in an integrated and planned manner.

Eklavya Model Residential School in Tribal Areas: These schools were opened by the government after the 9th Five-Year Plan for the children in tribal areas on the lines of Navodaya schools. The focus was to promote the need and importance of education among the tribals and at the same time strengthening the education infrastructure at the basic level to create opportunities for the future.

Skill Development Scheme for Tribal Communities: This focuses on improvement in livelihood standards by promotion of skills related to agriculture, livestock, fisheries, and non-farm activities. The skill upgradation provides the opportunities for employment/self-employment and also makes the tribal population aware of the market requirements and linkage.

Other Protective Measures for People Belonging to Tribal Areas in Himachal Pradesh: The Government of Himachal Pradesh has in place certain laws through which it ensures that the tribal people are not exploited by the wealthy people from outside or within the state. The state legislature has certain laws enacted to protect the people belonging to Scheduled Tribes which strengthens the control of these people over their land, resources, and properties. These laws and orders give the people protection from any outside interference and disturbance. Some of these areas follow:

Land Alienation: Under the Himachal Pradesh Transfer of Land (Regulation) Act, 1968, there is a provision which says that no person belonging to Scheduled Tribe in the state shall transfer his land including any constructed property by way of sale, mortgage, lease, gift to any person not belonging to such tribes except with the prior permission in writing from the State Government. This ensures that these people are not exploited by the influential person and the moneylenders. It serves as a protective mechanism against money and muscle power.

Himachal Pradesh Tenancy and Land Reform Act, 1972: This Act has ended all types of tenancy except under certain legal disabilities. In this case also the law provides for the *suo-motu* conferment of propriety rights on such tenants and they do not need to apply for the rights.

Provision of Scheduled Areas under Fifth Schedule of Constitution: In order to safeguard the interests of people belonging to the Scheduled Tribes, there are provisions given in the "Fifth Schedule" under article 244(2) of the Indian Constitution which identifies the areas with predominant tribal population and require special protection and measures for safeguarding the interests of population and culture. And it also talks about the administrative arrangement for the implementation of the policies and programmes in these areas.

Conclusion

From the study, we can conclude that decentralization as a concept for the development of local area is almost a few decades old now. The Institutionalisation for this happened with the 73rd Amendment Act, 1994, it provided a new soul to the development perspective. However, instead of all these efforts development and decentralization has not been penetrated to a level which was expected, in the tribal areas separate efforts were made with different provisions for these scheduled areas but the results are not on the expected lines. The reasons for this lag are many. There is a need for a paradigm shift in the approach. These areas need to be prioritized as It can act as a pool of talent and at the same time potential sites for development or tourism, sports, which in turn will help to generate revenue for the government. However, there is no denying the fact that efforts are continuously being made and fetching results also. As per the Socio-Economic Census of 2011, tribals of HP are in better condition as compared to Scheduled Tribe (ST) households in the rural areas of India. Nearly 22 per cent ST households have an income of more than Rs. 10,000 per month in the state and nearly 50 per cent tribal households own irrigated agricultural land. In getting the government sector jobs, the tribals in the state are ahead of other states with 23.72 per cent such households with at least one member in a government job. However, this does not represent the real picture of the Scheduled Tribes in Himachal Pradesh. The state's tribal areas have lower literacy rates as compared to the overall literacy in the state. They have less access to education, health facilities, basic infrastructure for development. So the development of these areas will take a leap once basic needs are fulfilled. The matter of the fact is that these areas need to be looked after by the government keeping in the backdrop of all the problems that these people face and making changes in the policies based upon the needs of the people in these areas. Need-based governance is the solution for their problems. The concept of one size fits all type of policies no longer exists, prioritization of problem areas is the key these days. And this is the area which should be strengthened in order to make that change in the development of these tribal areas look more visible and pragmatic.

References

4HPFFP-Tribal development Framework - Final.pdf (hpforest.nic.in)

Bhasin, Veena, (1996). *Transhumant of Himalayas*, Kamal Raj Enterprises, Delhi. Bose.

Bose, Nirmal K., (1972). *Some Indian Tribes*, National Book Trust, India, New Delhi.

Chakravarty, Sukhamoy (1987). *Development Planning: The Indian Experience*. Oxford University Press, Delhi.

Eleventh Five-year plan (2007-12) and Annual Tribal Sub-Plan (2009-10), Tribal Development Department, Government of Himachal Pradesh, Shimla.

Gupta, S.K., Sharma, V.P., Sharda, N.K. (1998). *Tribal Development, Appraisal and Alternatives*, Indus Publishing Company, New Delhi.

Handa, O.C., (2005). *Gaddi Land in Chamba: Its History, Art & Culture* (New Light on Early Wooden Temples), Indus Publishing Company, New Delhi.

Himachal Pradesh Forests for Prosperity Project (The World Bank assisted) Social Assessment & Management Framework—Tribal Development Framework—*Final Report.*

https://www.lkouniv.ac.in/site/writereaddata/siteContent/202004131501351340Neeti_ SW_Tribal_Community.pdf

Negi, T.S. (1976). Scheduled Tribes of Himachal Pradesh: A Profile, Raj printers, Meerut. Research report on "Utilization for Scheduled Tribes in Government Jobs (Central, State including PSUs)", Institute of Tribal Studies, H.P. University, Summer Hill, Shimla

Verma, V., (1996), *Gaddis of Dhauladhar—A Transhumant Tribe of the Himalayas*, Indus Publishing Company, New Delhi.

9

Decentralization and Selected Issues in Local-level Fiscal Decentralization

Priya Dahiya and *Rinki Dahiya*

Introduction

In modern democracy, decentralization has become an important dimension of governance. It has evolved as an adaptable practice across many countries and lack any precise definition at the practical realms. Generally, the term 'Decentralisation' is defined as a practice of the devolutions of political (functions), administrative (functionaries) and fiscal (finances) authorities, responsibilities and resources through deconcentration, delegation or devolution from central government to locally elected bodies in rural and urban areas for greater regional autonomy. In recent years, the subject of decentralization has received enthusiastic attention from academic analysts and policy-makers alike. Most analysts find inherent merit in decentralization like it promotes accountability, accessibility and effectiveness of the government. It delegates the decision-making power to the lower levels of the governments.

But by and large, practice of decentralisation in India is criticised due to its weak interface between political, administrative and fiscal decentralisation. These three degrees have not been congruently ensuing to the necessary extent and excessive state control on devolving the 3Fs is evident in majority of the states. Even when, in most of the states, political decentralisation takes place through the successive panchayat elections, the transfer of functionaries is still lagging behind in the transfer of functions and finances, and as is well-known, the transfer of functions by itself may not ensure progresses in provisioning of services. The under-supplied fiscal and administrative authorities to the PRIs from their respective states impede panchayats to implement and deliver the responsibilities entrusted upon them.

Fiscal Decentralization

The Central Government is increasingly finding difficulty to meet all of the numerous competing needs of their various constituencies at the regional and local levels. It is, therefore, attempting to build local capacity by delegating responsibilities downwards to their regional governments and local governments. At the same time, the local governments are also demanding more functional and financial autonomy. And want the taxation powers that commensurate with their expenditure responsibility.

Fiscal decentralization can be defined as transferring function and finances from higher level of government to the lower levels of governments through intergovernmental transfers and expenditure and revenue assignments. It is the process of analyzing the institutional structure and functioning of intergovernmental fiscal transfers in a federal set up. Intergovernmental fiscal transfers are intended to offset vertical and horizontal imbalances and bear significance especially when the fiscal autonomy of local level of governments is very sparse.

The traditional theories of fiscal decentralisation and its impact on service delivery; and within decentralisation setting, the role and performance of bureaucrats and politicians have been classified as first-generation theories (FGT) and second-generation theories (SGT). Qian and Weingast (1997), for the first time have dichotomised the fiscal decentralisation theories as FGT and SGT. The first-generation theories emphasised that it would be best that public service provisioning is assigned at decentralised tiers because of the proximity to citizens and their superior knowledge of revealed choices and preferences, while the national government should focus on macro-economic stabilisation and redistribution policies. The first-generation literature also focused on the revenue assignment structure in a multi-tier setup. The second-generation theories of fiscal decentralisation emphasised the political economy aspects and the institutional aspects of intertemporal budget constraint. The SGT emphasised on the public choice perspective of fiscal federalism, by focusing the behaviour of agents, who are in the process of providing services to the beneficiaries. Later, Oates (2005) succinctly presented a survey of fiscal federalism literature with such irreconcilable difference. Fiscal decentralisation has evolved as an adaptable practice across many countries and lacks precise definition at the practical realms. Many countries adapt different definition of decentralisation based on their demographic features, necessities for economic development especially pro-poor growth and development, government structure and so forth. Consequently, decentralised public management has been a longstanding debatable issue since its inception. Proponents of fiscal decentralisation consider it as a mechanism that has enormous potential in uplifting the overall public management of an economy, especially developing and emerging economies, while the other schools of thought consider it as a catastrophic step towards economic development of a nation.

In economic theory, there is an ample set of literature on fiscal decentralisation and its impact on growth, public service delivery, corruption, subnational public finance and overall human development, which have continued to generate debate. A large number of empirical literatures have evolved across various countries on the impact of decentralisation.

The concept, fiscal decentralisation caught attention of the various countries only after 1990. However, there are evidences that show that countries like Brazil, Peru and Mexico introduced a system of fiscal decentralisation in their economy in the 1990s. According to Kenneth Davey, fiscal decentralization covers two interrelated issues relating to division of spending and the amount of discretion to be given to regional and local governments to determine their expenditures and revenues.

Chio states that, fiscal decentralization means that the authority of tax collection or expenditure is transferred from superior to subordinate offices. He advocates that fiscal decentralisation has two aspects that is qualitative and quantitative. The qualitative aspect of fiscal decentralisation analyses finance held by a local government, whereas the quantitative aspect estimates the presence of autonomy authority in finance. According to N. Feruglio (2008), "fiscal decentralisation is a process of shifting decision-making power on the composition of expenditure responsibilities and on the composition and level of revenues from the Central Government to elected subnational governments". M.A. Oommen opined that "Fiscal decentralisation means fiscal empowerment of local governments. More specifically it means devolution of taxing and spending powers to lower levels of government."

According to Torres and Pachón (2013), any insignificant impact or negative impact of decentralisation on public service delivery may ensue unless there are: (1) well understanding and healthy relationship among all the three tiers of government, (2) political healthy competition in each tier, and (3) local politicians have comprehensive understanding of local needs. Tanzi's (1996) contribution in this area is in cautioning us that even in achieving allocative efficiency, a number of preconditions must be met for decentralization to be successful. The coordination requirements between different governmental levels are even more stringent with regard to achieving effective macroeconomic stabilization and the desired state of redistribution. The problems particularly severe in developing and transitional countries.

Using time series and cross section data for 85 countries, Huther and Shah (1998) and King and Ma (2001) concluded that fiscal decentralisation and macroeconomic management are positively associated since fiscal decentralisation has put up a better performance in bringing down fiscal deficits, public debts and controlling inflation. Huther and Shah (1998) have also shown that in all the 85 countries, decentralisation contributed in enhancing the delivery of public goods and services, ensuring quality of governance and reducing the level of corruption. In contrast, de Mello (2000), using a sample of 30 countries, revealed that fiscal decentralisation led to coordination failures among all the tiers of governments and consequently, deficit bias ensued. By analysing cross-country data, Triesman (2000) concluded that the incidences of corruption in a country increase, which has higher number of tiers of government as the likelihood of bribery increases. He also concluded that decentralisation impedes the public service delivery on pivotal sectors like health and education. Faguet (2001) found that in Bolivia, decentralisation has significantly improved quality and access of public services. However, in Argentina, Ravallion (1999) found that decentralisation has formed a substantial bias in public spending in other areas *vis-à-vis* poor areas of the country. On the contrary, Habibi *et al.* (2001) found that in Argentina, fiscal decentralisation contributed to improved delivery of education and health services and managed to reduce the level of intra-regional disparities as well. Several studies on China have also shown such kind of mixed results related to the impact of decentralisation.

In Indian context, mixed results on the impact of fiscal decentralisation process have been observed. Wade (1997) found incompatibility between bottom-up demand and top-down management and poor communication among the tiers of government due to the over-centralised top-down management that resulted in corruption and insubstantial service delivery for canal irrigation in India. Mahal and Rajaraman (2010) and Rajaraman (2014) found that fiscal decentralisation has not led to improved public service delivery on education and health. Rodriguez-Pose and Bwire (2003) empirically investigated the horizontal link between devolution and regional economic growth for six countries including India and found that devolution has no impact for India. In this regard, Rao and Singh (1998), Rao (2004), and Rao *et al.* (2011) examined why fiscal decentralisation is falling short in effectively delivering overall public services, and found that discretionary transfers are generally skewed towards the states with higher income while formula-based transfers from Finance Commission help in offsetting vertical and horizontal imbalances.

In keeping with the global pattern, in India too there has been a trend towards greater devolution of powers to urban and rural local governments particularly since the 1990s. Of course, attempts to decentralise the administrative system and establishment of self-governing institutions has much longer history and there have been sporadic attempts at devolving powers and rights to rural and urban local governments, particularly after Independence. However, the impetus gained momentum with the statutory recognition of local bodies as institutions of rural and urban self-government after the 73rd and 74th Constitutional Amendments in 1992. Until this development, India evolved as a two-tiered federal structure with the powers and functions demarcated between the Union and the States. Although this was done not as a component of structural reform, the attempt to decentralise allocative decisions was in conformity with the change in the development strategy towards a more open and market-friendly economic regime.

The Government of India after several decades of deliberation introduced two Constitutional Amendments—the 73rd Amendment (rural decentralization) and 74th Amendments (urban decentralization)—to give effect to its objectives of decentralization. In 1992, 73rd and 74th Constitutional Amendments were enacted, which entrusted the state governments to pass appropriate legislation to promote self-governance through statutory recognition of local bodies. These two amendments were intended to reinforce public service deliver in a greater detail through improved decentralized governance. But even before that, several commissions and committees were constituted for fiscal decentralization, suggesting various measures to strengthen fiscal autonomy of Panchayats and Municipalities.

However, the Panchayati Raj Institution (PRI) structure failed to steer adequate rural development despite putting into force the recommendations of Balwant Rai Mehta Committee (1957) and Ashoka Mehta Committee (1977). The Balwant Rai Mehta Committee recommended the block as the unit of planning with the Panchayat Samitis as the executive body for planning. Ashok Mehta Committee considered inadequacy of resources, mainly responsible for failure of PR is and, therefore, recommended, inter alia, measures for strengthening the financial resources of PR is. In 1986, the L.M. Singhvi Committee recommended constitutional status for PRIs is with Gram Sabha as the basic unit. In India, constitutional status to local governments has been provided in 1992 by 73rd and 74th Constitutional Amendments (for rural and urban areas respectively), which came into force in 1993. It has entrusted the state governments to pass appropriate legislation to promote self-governance through statutory recognition of local bodies. So, one might expect that the goals the government wants to achieve with fiscal decentralization are better local public services, increased revenue mobilization, a more efficient use of public money, and more involvement of people in the process of their governance.

Generally, it is considered that a representative government functions in a better manner, when it is close to the people. And fiscal federalism encourages participation of locals at the grassroots level and bring government closer to the people. It is always argued that the fiscal federalism is an optimal institutional arrangement as it ensures fiscal responsibility to the lower level of government (local self-government) and this leads to good governance, which promotes accountability, responsiveness, political participation, and diversity.

So, there are number of reasons for analyzing fiscal federalism in India. First of all, from economic point of view, fiscal federalism helps to combine the advantages of decentralization with economies of scale benefits and this result in providing public services with minimum cost for maximum welfare. And thereby it promotes economic value. It is also argued that with fiscal decentralization funds are efficiently utilized through the need-based and demand-driven approach. So, it carefully targets the low-income segment of the society.

Secondly, Fiscal decentralization is supposed to provide a forum for local debates relating to the local priorities and enhances political participation at the local level. It places greater emphasis on transparency and accountability. As a result, it has the potential to enhance political stability and democratic values at the local level. That is why India is very much in favour of fiscal decentralization because it places decision making close to the people.

But there are several reasons why the present system falls short of meeting these goals. This chapter points to several problem areas, including expenditure assignments, local autonomy over budgets, fiscal role of the Gram Panchayats, the transfer system, fiscal pressures and revenue efforts by Gram Panchayats.

Further, relatively little has been done to unbundle the general subjects prescribed in the Constitution, and make expenditure assignments at a more detailed level of activity and sub-activity. As a result, there is an unclear assignment of expenditures between the three tiers that has led to duplication of efforts, some failure to assume leadership in the delivery of services, coordination problems and some uncertainty on the part of the local population as to where accountability lies.

One major constraint to true fiscal decentralization is the limited expenditure discretion that has been given to the local governments. Even though a significant portion of public expenditures are being channeled through panchayats, in effect expenditures actually controlled by local governments are well less than 10 per cent of total rural spending by local bodies. The lack of independent sources of revenue and total dependence of ZPs and TPs on transfers makes the entire fiscal decentralization process for these levels hostage to the transfer system. There are almost no general purpose transfers at the district and block levels. The scheme-based devolution and micro allocation of resources even within the schemes do not provide any leeway to the districts and taluks in making allocation decisions according to their priorities. In fact, the entire fiscal decentralization process has ensured that the district and block panchayats are mere disbursing agents of the higher-level governments. However, Gram Panchayats, because they have own source of revenues, and because they receive their transfers more in the form of unconditional transfers, do have more discretion to allocate expenditures to meet local needs. It is estimated that they have complete authority to allocate about one-third of their budgets, and limited control over expenditures of another one-third.

The higher-level governments retained most powers to hire, fire and compensate local government employees, hence Panchayati Raj Institutions (PRIs) have relatively little control over their personnel budgets. The role of the Gram Panchayats (GPs) in rural local finance is quite small. Yet, the Gram Panchayat is arguably the best choice for local autonomy given that this tier of government is closest to the people and the fact that it has some taxing power.

The analysis shows that the level of expenditures incurred at the GP level is extremely low both in per capita terms and as a per cent of gross domestic product. Even as a ratio of total expenditure of rural local governments, the role of GPs is quite limited. In addition, overwhelming proportions of expenditures are incurred for specific purposes such as JGSY, welfare of Scheduled Castes, and salaries. Of course, these are necessary, but it is worth noting that they are directed to benefit a small section of the population within the GPs. The activities of GPs do not evoke appreciable interest and response from the majority of people.

Revenue effort by Gram Panchayats is weak and own source revenues are negligible. A number of reasons have been suggested for this weak revenue performance:

- An unwillingness of the local officials to enforce the tax laws.
- The limited capacity of local government officials to effectively administer a revenue system.

- Weak administration procedures, for example, tax rolls are not maintained, assessments are not done in a scientific way and are not updated, and collection procedures are not efficient.
- The need for more productive bases to tax.
- Local officials have little incentive to raise additional taxes.

Transfer system is complicated, non-transparent, and non-equalizing and conditional grants to rural local governments from the State and the Centre, and it is difficult to coordinate these or monitor their effectiveness. Because, the conditions on the expenditure of these grant funds are so restrictive, local governments have little opportunity to structure local expenditure to match local preferences. A small portion of the total grant funds is given to Gram Panchayats as untied aid, and this does provide some measure of local discretion. It would not be far off the mark to say that the present system of inter-governmental transfers is inconsistent with the goal of developing fiscal decentralization in the rural local government sector.

So, overall a major shortcoming in Indian fiscal system is its lack of attention to fiscal issues at local levels, particularly in rural areas. Very little is known about the public finances of Panchayati Raj Institutions and the fiscal relationship between state and local governments.

Serious thought must be given to introduce institutional reforms that promote accountability, transparency, and efficiency. It seems necessary to clearly define the basis of fiscal devolution among the different tiers of government (centre, state, and local government) which result in fiscal collaboration rather than confrontation and promote healthy and cordial economic relation among them.

There is a need to bring in mainstream accounting by the introduction of journal-ledger, budgets and audits. The accounting system and the manner of presentation of the budgets should be redesigned in such a manner that appropriate financial reporting is made possible for various purposes, such as ongoing monitoring, performance evaluation, or cost of providing individual services. For keeping up-to-date accounts and for ensuring transparency, it is necessary to computerize the bookkeeping function of Panchayats.

Building and maintaining a reliable information system is key to designing and implementing an efficient inter-governmental fiscal system. All efforts should be made to assure regional fiscal equality by allocating funds on the criteria of equality and efficiency. Fiscal decentralization can be strengthened by restructuring tax responsibility to allow local revenue autonomy and accountability by delegating the responsibility to the local level to collect and spend tax according to the local needs.

Conclusion

Even 30 years after the Constitutional Amendment, the agenda and implementation plan for rural local government finance is not clear. Some states burdened the district and the block levels with state personnel and earmarked the use of resources such that elected governments are treated as service agents. The tier closest to the people, the Gram Panchayat, has been left with hardly any resource and very little expenditure discretion.

Despite India's commitment to rural decentralization, Panchayats cannot live up to their potential because the structure of the fiscal decentralization system is flawed. While states continue to make efforts on moving ahead on this policy agenda, what is in place today is a patchwork of legislation and measures that reflect what has been politically and bureaucratically possible. While many initiatives have tried to move the agenda forward, they were pursued in a fragmented and narrow way.

References

Bagchi A. (2003). "Fifty Years of Fiscal Federalism in India: An Appraisal", *Working Paper 2*, National Institute of Public Finance and Policy, New Delhi.

Bagchi, A., and P. Chakraborty (2004). "Towards a Rational System of Centre-State Revenue Transfer". *Economic and Political Weekly, 39*(26): 2737-47.

Bahl, R. (2002). "Implementation Rules for Fiscal Decentralisation". In *Development, Poverty and Fiscal Policy: Decentralisation of Institutions* (Ed.) M. Govinda Rao. Oxford University Press, New Delhi.

Bahl, R., and J. Linn (1994). "Fiscal Decentralization and Intergovernmental Transfers in Less Developed Countries". *Publius, 24*(1): 1-19.

Chakraborty, P. (2008). "Budget Rules, Fiscal Consolidation and Government Spending: Implications for Federal Transfers". *MPRA Paper* No. *30938.*

Chakraborty, P., L. Chakraborty, and A. N. Mukherjee (2016). *Social Sector in a Decentralized Economy: India in the Era of Globalization.* Cambridge University Press, New Delhi.

Faguet, J.P. (2001). "Does Decentralization Increase Responsiveness to Local Needs? Evidence from Bolivia". *Policy Research Working Paper 2516*: The World Bank, Washington, D.C.

Fukasaku Kiichiro and L.R. De Mello, Jr. (1999). *Fiscal Decentralization in Emerging Economies.* Development Centre, OECD, Paris.

Gramlich, E.M. and H. Galper (1973). State and Local Fiscal Behavior and Federal Grant Policy, *Brookings Papers Econ. Activity, 1*: 15-58.

Huther, J. and A. Shah (1998). "Applying a Simple Measure of Good Governance to the Debate on Fiscal Decentralization". *Policy Research Working Paper Number 1894*: World Bank, Washington, D.C.

Inman, R.P. (1979). "The Fiscal Performance of Local Governments: An Interpretative Review". In *Current Issues in Urban Economics* (ed.) P. Mieszkowski and M. Staszheim., Baltimore: John Hopkins University Press.

Jha, Shikha (2002). "Strengthening Local Governments: Rural Fiscal Decentralization in India", *Economic and Political Weekly*, Vol. 37, No. 26.

Oates, Wallace E. (2006). On Theory and Practice of Fiscal Decentralisation, *IFIR Working Paper*, Series No. 2006-05, Revised draft.

Oommen, M.A. (2005). "Rural Fiscal Decentralisation in India: A Brief Review of Literature", quoted in L.C. Jain (ed) (2005): *Decentralisation and Local Governance: Essays for George Mathew*, Orient Longman Private Limited, New Delhi.

Parker, A.N. (1995). "Decentralization: The Way Forward for Rural Development?" *Policy Research Working Paper No. 1475*, The World Bank.

Rao, M.G. and N. Singh. 2005. *Political Economy and Federalism in India.* New Delhi: Oxford University Press.

Rao, M.G. (2006). "Resolving Fiscal Imbalances: Issues in Revenue Sharing. In Intergovernmental Fiscal Transfers" (ed.) R. Boadway and A. Shah., 319-338. The World Bank, Washington D.C.

Rodden, J. (2003). *Reviving Leviathan: Fiscal Federalism and the Growth of Government.* International Organization.

Rodríguez-Pose, A. and A. Bwire (2003). *The Economic (in) Efficiency of Devolution.* Department of Geography and Environment, London School of Economics.

Tanzi, V. (1996). Fiscal Federalism and Decentralization: A Review of Some Efficiency and Macroeconomic Aspects. *Annual World Bank conference on development economics,* 295-316. World Bank, Washington, D.C.

Shah, A., T. Thompson, and H. Zou (2004). "The Impact of Decentralisation on Service Delivery, Corruption, Fiscal Management and Growth in Developing and Emerging Market Economies: A Synthesis of Empirical Evidence". *CESifo DICE Report.*

10

Challenges of Decentralization in Rural Development

Kanhaiya Lal

Decentralization is a popular concept and a system in which the transfer of power and resources takes place at different levels—from the centre to the village unit, and each level, being independent and self-accountable in its own place for its activities, remains connected to the centre. In decentralization, participation of local people at various levels is ensured in planning, implementation, and monitoring of programmes for development. Decentralization is the system in which the power is in the hands of the people and the government works for the development of the people, it is influenced by the transfer of responsibility for decision making, management or allocation of resources from the higher level of government to its local units.[1]

The direct participation of local people in planning and implementation under decentralization provides an opportunity to understand the needs and priorities of the people and to empower the weaker sections. Panchayati Raj system in India is known as a major instrument of decentralization through which democracy becomes truly representative and accountable. Before the 73rd

Constitutional Amendment, Indian states were functioning at only two levels—Union and State, but after the 73rd Constitutional Amendment, powers have been given from the states to the local bodies by strengthening the process of decentralization in India.[2] Decentralization is significantly useful as a political process by which administrative authority, public resources, and responsibilities are transferred from Central Government agencies to various units at lower levels of government.[3] Democratic Decentralization is a process whereby the functions and resources of the state are devolved from the Centre to the Elected Representatives at the Lower Level to ensure greater participation of citizens in the Governance System.[4] The devolution of powers in three areas has been considered essential in many studies for the success of Decentralisation. This Political, Administrative, and Financial Decentralization can manifest in various forms and combinations within countries and even across regions. The purpose of Political Decentralization is to give more power to the citizens or their elected representatives in Decision-Making. This opportunity is associated with representative government but it supports Democratic Decentralization by giving citizens or their representatives more influence in the formulation and implementation of policies. Financial Decentralization involves the transfer of financial resources in the form of grants and tax-raising powers to Local Units of Government. Under Administrative Decentralization, the functions performed by the Central Government are geographically transferred to different Administrative Units.

The socio-economic status of the citizens and the progress of the society largely depend on the Good Governance at the grassroots level. The concept of Democratic Decentralization at the grassroots level to make democracy meaningful and responsible, corruption-free, effective, and Democratic Decentralization for rural and urban population is widely recognized as an important political instrument and means balanced and equitable development in Indian States. Better and faster communication through Decentralization of power, people's participation and commitment in Development, greater support for National Development and utilization of resources, improving Decision Making Process (reducing delays) allocation of resources and investments. At the same time, transparent administration and delivery of services towards citizens is the most important and useful strategy to achieve the larger goals.[5] The concept of Decentralization is based on the practices and traditions developed over the years. The basic framework of inter-governmental relations in the Indian Union is given by the constitutional provisions of functions and sources of finance. In the Seventh Schedule to the Constitution of India—the jurisdiction of the Central Government on the Union List, the jurisdiction of the States on the State List, and the jurisdiction of both the States and the Union on the Concurrent List.

An important feature of constitutional work in India is the centripetal bias in the division of powers. First, almost all broad-based taxes, with the sole exception of sales tax, are delegated to the Central Government. Second, effectively, States do not have independent borrowing power. When a state is indebted to the Centre, it must seek the Centre's permission to borrow as all states are indebted to the Centre, their market borrowings as determined by the Union Finance Ministry in consultation with the scheme. Realizing the potential benefits of decentralization in the Indian federation has been hindered by factors and various financial and regulatory barriers to the movement of producers across the country. Some of these barriers were created for the economic management of the lack of supply of essential commodities. The fiscal constraints were a result of the free ride behaviour of the State specifically attempting to export the tax burden to non-residents. These constraints, along with a high level of security, distorted relative prices and created a high-cost economy.

Two important things emerge from the above analysis. First, the potential economic benefits of Decentralization in the Indian Union could not be achieved because of the concentrated bias in the Constitution and the centralization of economic powers due to planning and other developments. Second, there has been a significant inter-state variation in the degree of Decentralization and other institutional conditions. This has had different effects on the states. Therefore, it is necessary to have a better understanding of the economic dynamics of Decentralization from the analysis of different states. Another important feature of Indian financial federalism is the existence of severe vertical and horizontal imbalances (Rao, 2009). States have been entrusted with expenditure responsibilities far exceeding their revenue resources. Specifically, the constitution entrusts the states with the prime responsibility of building social and physical infrastructure for rural development. In addition, the revenue mobilization capacity appears to vary widely across states in India.[6]

Concept of Rural Development

Rural areas can be defined from the point of view of their circumstances, economy and Political Administration (Hoggart, 1990; Beginnings & Procter, 2001). Ecologically, the landscape of Rural areas consists mainly of fields, forests, rivers or mountains, where it is scattered with minimal physical infrastructure. Economically, most of the Rural People are engaged in agriculture, animal husbandry, forestry and fisheries, which somehow shows a high incidence of poverty. While Rural areas are relatively easy to be identified from the circumstances and economic point of view, it is more clearly defined from the Political Administrative point of view. There is a clear distinction between Rural and Urban, as economic change has created suburban areas, where the characteristics of Rural and Urban are mixed.

Thus, Rural Development is defined as the overall development programmes conducted mainly in rural areas. Ellis and Biggs (2001) state that until the 1970s, Rural Development was primarily referred to as Agricultural Development aimed at promoting grain production. In order to broaden the concept of Rural Development, its three main elements are mentioned. First, most of the literature agrees that Rural Development is a multi-sectoral programme covering not only agriculture but also infrastructure, microfinance, environment, human resources etc. Second, Rural Development aims to improve the quality of life of villagers by access to Income, Housing, Education, Health and other Public Services. Third, although Rural Development targets the Rural Community as a whole, much of the literature agrees that it should give priority to the poorest group (Ellis and Biggs, 2001; Fernando, 2008; Singh, 1999; World Bank, 1975).

Poverty alleviation is the main objective of Rural Development. The literature broadly defines poverty as the lack of basic necessities to maintain an adequate standard of livings (Houghton & Khandkar, 2009). Poverty is measured by setting the poverty line, which is a person's minimum calorie intake and the minimum level of income needed to make a better living through other services. The World Bank set the poverty line at US$2 per day for Moderate Poverty and US$1 per day for Extreme Poverty. Poverty has many dimensions (Houghton and Khandkar, 2009; Ravelian, 1996). Therefore, a simple measure based on income alone cannot fully describe the nature of poverty. Henry, Sharma, Lapenu and Zeller (2001) view that a Relative Poverty State can be identified by the amount of Food consumed, Housing conditions, Property ownership, Education and Expenditure. Although this method is still not able to measure the multiple dimensions of Poverty, it provides a relatively easy way to identify the poor in a community.[7]

Democratic Decentralization in Rural Areas

After Independence, Rural Development became the cornerstone of India's Development Strategy. The main objective of Rural Development Programmes is to improve the standard of living of the Rural People by providing them opportunities for better utilization of their potentials through active participation of the people in the Development Process. Development programmes have a better chance of success when Rural People participate in various stages of the Developmental Decision-Making Process. In the year 1992, through the 73rd Constitutional Amendment, the Government of India gave constitutional recognition to Panchayati

Raj Institutions with the objective of making Rural people a participant in the Decision-Making Process of Development and improving participation in Decentralized Planning.[8]

Adequate and proper participation of local people is essential for successful Rural Development. Local people's participation is an important factor in the success of Infrastructure Development, Micro Finance, Capacity Development, Agricultural Extension, Education and Health reforms and Government Programmes. Community participation contributes to the success of the programme through increased resource mobilization, providing checks and balances, improving the matching between Development outcomes and Rural people's needs. Decentralization, particularly by Devolution to Local Government, is expected to provide the maximum possible space for participation. This is because the Local Government is closer to the people than the Central Government. This type of transfer minimizes the time and distance cost to negotiate with the Government. As observed by Cheema and Rondinelli (2007), Decentralization not only provides more space for people to participate in Local Representative selection, but also in the context of wider Local Development. A review by Blair (2000) in the six countries of Bolivia, Honduras, India, Mali, Philippines and Ukraine found that although the Decentralized System still has limitations in promoting participation, at least it provides opportunity to marginalized groups to enter Politics. This is because Political Decentralization provides for local representation and a system for electing leaders. When minorities are allotted some seats in the Local Legislature, they can work for the interest of their groups. Blair also found that increased representation provided benefits in itself. A local election process that guarantees people's rights to choose their leaders may at least be a means to make government more accountable.

Administrative Decentralization occurs when the Central Government transfers public sector functions to institutions outside the Local Government or Bureaucracy. Administrative Decentralization increases government accountability because it enables people to supervise their Local Authorities (Braun & Groot, 2009). Cohen and Peterson (1997) argue that increasing the number of institutions providing services will not only increase accountability, but also make service delivery better managed and tailored to local needs. Administrative Decentralization, mainly by involving Local Institutions in implementing government programmes, provides an opportunity to apply institutional approaches to Poverty Alleviation (Braun & Groot, 2009; Cohen & Peterson, 1997). These institutions should be empowered through Financial and Technical assistance, so that they can be able to provide better service to the Rural People. Various development programmes have been implemented in many countries emphasizing the roles of Local Institutions. The programme of Rural Community Forestry in Nepal is an example of a success story of institutional approach in Local Resource Management. In this country, the government delegates forest conservation tasks to Local Community Organizations. The Local Community, which knows the condition of the forest better and is heavily dependent on it as a source of livelihood, is able to use the forest in a sustainable manner.[9]

Challenges of Decentralization

There are many Challenges and Obstacles towards the progress of Decentralization. Due to insufficient funds given by the Central Government to the Local Governments, the Local Governments are not able to solve the Local Problems and meet the Basic Needs. There is little investment in enabling Local Governments to raise their own taxes and user charges. There is an acute shortage of staff for performing basic functions with Local Governments. With most employees being hired by Higher Level Departments and on Deputation with Local Governments, they feel no responsibility for the latter. The Elections of Local Units are not held regularly and on time. Local Governments are acting only as an Implementation Unit rather than a Policy Making Body of Local Development. Criminal instincts and contractors are attracted to

Local Government Elections, who are now lured by the large sums of money flowing to them. Corruption is also a major challenge in which there is participation between Elected Representatives and officials at all levels. Although there is no evidence to show that decentralization has led to corruption. Decentralized corruption is exposed faster than corruption at the national or state level. People mistakenly perceive high corruption at the local level, simply because it is more visible. However, it is here that representatives of corrupt local government can be more easily tracked than those at higher levels.[10]

Most of the states have not devolved adequate funds and functions to these bodies despite fulfilling the necessary conditions like enactment of State Panchayat Act, setting up of State Finance Commission and State Election Commission and constitution of District Planning Committee etc. Some states like Kerala and West Bengal have transferred 26 departments to panchayats. Many states have transferred only certain functions. Article 243G of the Constitution of India, which requires state governments to assign different functional items to panchayats, is still a constitutional promise. For example, the "Expert Committee for More Efficient Delivery of Public Goods and Services to Panchayati Raj Institutions" revealed that except the Mahatma Gandhi National Rural Employment Guarantee Act (MGNREGA) and the Backward Regions Grant Fund (BRGF), none. These are still managed by the respective departments of the respective states. That is, panchayats are yet to develop into fully self-governing institutions of local government, due to continued resistance from the political leadership and certain sections of the bureaucracy, who feel that the rise of panchayats will supersede them.

The more worrying trend is that despite two decades, much of the efforts made to strengthen the functioning and delivery capacity of these institutions are insufficient. While only a few states have done little to internalize the planning process of panchayats, many have not given any serious attention to building the capacities of newly elected representatives, many of whom are first-time MPs.

Therefore, the lack of capacity has taken a toll on the credibility of this very promising institution. It is not surprising that many elected representatives are completely dependent on officials to perform basic responsibilities, which often become the subject of ridicule. This is more evident in the poorest and backward regions, where it is extremely difficult for elected representatives to perform well in implementing rural development plans. This lack of capacity is being used as a clever excuse by the political and bureaucratic leadership to delegate multiple functions to these bodies, with the situation even more dire in the case relating to the PESA Act (Fifth Scheduled Areas).[11]

Decentralization requires strong financial capacity of the Local Government. The Central Government usually transfers some amount required to carry out the delegated functions. Nevertheless, in addition to receiving financial transfers from the Central Government, the Local Government must have its own capacity to generate Local Revenue. There may be several options for generating Local Revenue, such as setting up Locally Managed Enterprises, using Natural Resources and collecting Local Taxes (Lewis, 2003; Livingston and Charlton, 2001). Nevertheless, Local Government is known for its low ability to manage business. The easiest way to generate revenue is through the continuous extraction of Natural Resources and the progressive increase in Local Taxes.

In order to be successful in promoting institutional approaches in Poverty Alleviation, Decentralized Programmes must be implemented by institutions of sufficient capacity. Nevertheless, there are many concerns that local institutions may not have sufficient capacity. UNDP (2002) in its report on Capacity Development Programmes conducted around the World concluded that successful and Sustainable Capacity Development still cannot be achieved, and despite training thousands of people, the lack of skills and weak institutions still remains large. There is a problem. Furthermore, Johnson (2001) states that the local capacity is probably reduced due to the long application of top-down development. He also expressed concern that Poverty in Rural

Areas could undermine the ability of local people to participate in Decentralisation. The low Education level of Rural people can hinder their ability to understand Government Policy. If the poor do not participate in Decision Making, they may not benefit from Decentralisation.[12] Institutional capacity building at the Local Level requires continuous Economic and Technical support by the Central Government, which is often lacking.[13]

At this time of governance collapse, alarming level of erosion in the institutional integrity, scams and angry protests, one hopes to see certain degree of urgency and seriousness from the political leadership and policy makers to walk the talk on the devolution and decentralization as promised in the 73rd Amendment. Mere constitutional creation of new political space would not become the answer to the growing demands for inclusion and participation in the countryside. For substantive democracy to become a reality, Centre and States need to show willingness to share powers.[14] The Centre and the states need to work with mutual cooperation and coordination by empowering the Local Units and giving more powers to the states to make Democracy successful.

Suggestion

Better Research Results and Policy Experience can help policy-makers to implement reforms in Decentralization. When properly designed and implemented, there is evidence that Decentralization Policies have many benefits, ranging from better Public Service Delivery and greater Citizen Engagement to less corruption and a positive impact on Rural Development. Access to finance should be commensurate with functional responsibilities. The formula for devolution of government grants and earmarked funds from the central to the lower levels of government should be transparent and non-discretionary.[15] The Ministry of Panchayati Raj should monitor the release of grants and expenditure of the Finance Commission to ensure that there should be no delay in his release. It should also be ensured that the grants are utilized in an appropriate and effective manner.[16]

The Central Government should assess the capacity challenges in various sectors on a regular basis and make efforts towards addressing them. In order to strengthen the capabilities, emphasis should be laid on adapting the Policies to the different needs of the regions. Governments should strive to strengthen the capacities of public officials and institutions in a systematic approach rather than with limited focus on technical assistance. Staff training should be established in the basics of Local Public Financial Management. Open, competitive recruitment and merit-based promotion must be ensured. Rural-Urban partnerships should be promoted as a form of Cross-Jurisdictional collaboration to drive inclusive growth by bringing about multi-benefits. Citizens should be empowered through access to information. Ensure that elected local units own and control citizen participation and participatory initiatives. Continuously improve transparency, increase data collection and strengthen performance monitoring. The Central Government is required to monitor Sub-National performance in critical service areas based on a minimum set of standardized indicators and provide timely feedback as well as benchmark Inter-Local performance in service delivery. In order to achieve the objective of people's participation in real terms[17] Gram Sabhas and Ward Committees have to be revived. The Standing Committee on Rural Development, which submitted its report in July 2018, recommended that "State governments should complete the quorum in Gram Sabha meetings for the participation of Panchayat representatives, including women." The organizational structure of the Local Government with adequate manpower has to be strengthened. Serious efforts should be made for Recruitment and Appointment of Support and Technical Staff to ensure smooth functioning of Panchayats. Create a Comprehensive Mechanism for Taxation at the Local Level. There is a need for bottom-up planning, especially at the District Level, based on the ground inputs received from the Gram Sabha. The Empowerment of Panchayats should be given more impetus through capacity building and training from the Central and State Governments. This will enable them to prepare better Gram Panchayat Development Plans as well as become more responsible for meeting the needs of the Citizens.[18]

Conclusion

Decentralized Governance is a System that makes people's participation in Administration and Development Programmes possible and successful. Decentralized Governance is a strategy to exercise equal rights for all people and a means of capacity building for Rural Development. Decentralization is widely appreciated as a key component of Good Governance and Development. Decentralization and Democracy can improve the chances of successful Rural Development. Decentralization is one of the best efforts to reduce Poverty and promote Sustainable Development in India. The passing of the 73rd Constitutional Amendment in 1992 was an important step in this direction. Identifying Panchayati Raj Institutions (PRIs) as agents of Local Self-government and entrusted them with the responsibility of formulating plans for promoting Rural Development and Social Justice. While most states ratified the 73rd Amendment to state acts and held Elections, the quality of Political, Administrative and Financial Decentralization varied widely from State to State. States have not matched the functions assigned to Local Government Institutions with the necessary Administrative Reforms, or by Devolution of Financial Powers. As a result, there is neither the ability to implement the assigned tasks that substantively remain under the control of the State Administration nor do they have control over the resources to take relevant decisions. The 73rd Amendment should be more practical to strengthen the Decentralization Process. Without proper Popular Representation, local interests will not be protected and local initiatives will not receive the required level of support. Unnecessary interference by Bureaucrats, Political Leaders and Members of Parliament must be stopped. The relationship between Parliamentarians and Local Government should be cooperative and complementary, not domination and subordination.

However, progress on Fiscal and Functional Decentralization has been mixed. There are several states that have taken steps to transfer funds and functions to Panchayati Raj Institutions. The process of transfer is at different stages of operation in different states. The states of Kerala, Madhya Pradesh and Uttar Pradesh, which have little experience in Decentralization, have made the most fundamental changes in this regard. In addition, it is essential that the Panchayati Raj Institutions have the resources to fulfill the responsibilities assigned to them. While State Finance Commissions have submitted their recommendations, very few States have taken necessary steps to ensure the financial viability of Panchayati Raj Institutions. Nevertheless, it can be expected that the experience of some PRIs within some states and states will provide the necessary impetus for Greater Devolution to other parts of the Country.

Nores

1. https://www.orfonline.org/research/even-after-20-years-decentralization -still remains-a-challenge/
2. https://www.researchgate.net/publication/329415345_democratic_decentralization_in_india_an_overview
3. https://odi.org/en/publications/decentralization-in-india-poverty-politics-and-panchayati-raj/
4. https://www.drishtiias.com/daily-updates/daily-news-editorials/democratic-decentralization-in-india
5. https://www.researchgate.net/publication/329415345_democratic_decentralization_in_india_an_overview
6. https://crawford.anu.edu.au/acde/asarc/pdf/papers/2010/WP2010_14.pdf
7. http://eprints.ipdn.ac.id/176/1/decentralization%2C%20%20potentialities%20and%20challenge%20for%20rural20development.pdf
8. https://egyankosh.ac.in/handle/123456789/25850
9. http://eprints.ipdn.ac.id/176/1/decentralization%2C%20%20potentialities%20and%20challenge%20for%20rural%20development.pdf
10. https://www.drishtiias.com/daily-updates/daily-news-editorials/democratic-decentralization-in-india

11. https://www.orfonline.org/research/even-after-20-years-decentralization-still remains-a-challenge/
12. http://eprints.ipdn.ac.id/176/1/decentralization%2C%20%20potentialities%20and%20challenge%20for%2 0 r u r a l % 2 0 development.pdf
13. https://www.gov.br/cgu/pt-br/acesso-a-informacao/institucional/eventos/anos-anteriores/2005/iv-forum-global-de-combate-a-corrupcao-1/arquivos/nickdevas-2.pdf
14. https://www.orfonline.org/research/even-after-20-years-decentralization -still remains-a-challenge/
15. https://www.oecd.org/regional/making-decentralization-work-g2g9faa7-en.htm.
16. https://www.drishtiias.com/daily-updates/daily-news-editorials/democratic-decentralization-in-india
17. https://www.oecd.org/regional/making-decentralization-work-g2g9faa7-en.htm.
18. https://www.drishtiias.com/daily-updates/daily-news-editorials/democratic-decentralization-in-india

11

Challenges to Decentralization and Tribal Development through E-Governance

Vikram Prashant and *Umesh Kumar*

Introduction

Tribes are a social group comprising numerous families, clans, or generations together, a group of persons having a common character, occupation, or interest. We can define a tribe as a social group with territorial affiliation, endogamous with no specialization of functions ruled by tribal officers hereditary or otherwise, united in language or dialect recognizing social distance with other tribes or castes. The term "tribal society" is used to refer to societies organized largely based on social, especially familial, descent groups (such as clan and kinship). A customary tribe in these terms is a face-to-face community, relatively bound by kinship relations, reciprocal exchange, and strong ties to place. Technology, policy, and governance are all intricately intertwined in a variety of ways. We need citizen participation in order for these three things to function well. Policies that are centered on the individual, and open technology that will lead to good governance. A good governance system should include elements such as efficiency, effectiveness, transparency, responsiveness, accountability, which is supported once more by concepts such as equity, consensus, and the rule of law as well as inclusivity. E-Governance is a stepping stone towards good governance, and it is all about transformation. People, process, technology, and business model are the four pillars of e-governance, as sustainability is critical. Decentralized governance has been conceived as an instrument in promoting development and e-governance can contribute to decentralization. In realizing the rights of the tribals, the Constitution of India has provided special provisions by delineating special administrative structures for tribal development with enacting the Fifth and the Sixth Schedules. The Sixth Schedule is applicable to four states of north-east India, namely Assam, Meghalaya, Tripura, and Mizoram, and the Fifth Schedule is in operation in other regions of the country where tribes form a majority in a district or districts. The Sixth Schedule provides for autonomous district councils, thus offering space for tribal self-governance.

Common Problem Faced by Tribes

1. **Loss of Control over Natural Resources:** Prior to the arrival of the British, tribals had unrestricted ownership and management of natural resources such as land, forests, wildlife, water, soil, fish etc. With the arrival of industrialization in India and the discovery of mineral and other resources in tribal inhabited areas, these pockets were opened up to outsiders, and state control replaced tribal control. Thus began the plot of the tribals' never-ending agony and pain. With the impetus to the development process that came with independence, the pressure on land and forests increased. Due to long-term indebtedness, dishonest landlords, moneylenders, contractors, and officials, this resulted in the loss of land ownership rights. The native tribes felt uprooted from their local cultures and without a secure means of livelihood as the concepts of protected forests and national forests gained importance.

2. **Lack of Education:** According to the 2011 Census, nearly 50 per cent of the tribal people are illiterate. Although it cannot be denied that education can be a valuable tool for tribal people's betterment, facilitating participation in the development process, there are certain barriers that prevent tribal people from pursuing education. Among these factors are tribal superstitions and prejudices, extreme poverty, the nomadic lifestyle of certain tribes, a loss of enthusiasm in alien subjects taught in an alien language, and a lack of suitable teachers and other amenities in tribal areas.
3. **Displacement and Rehabilitation:** Post-Independence, the emphasis of the development process shifted to heavy industries and the core sector. As a result, massive steel plants, power projects, and large dams sprouted up, the majority of which were in tribal inhabited areas. Mining activities in these areas have also been accelerated. The government's acquisition of tribal land for these projects led to substantial displacement of the tribal population. The tribal pockets of Chhotanagpur, Orissa, West Bengal, and Madhya Pradesh have been severely impacted. The government's monetary compensation was depleted on wasteful spending. There were no settlements for the displaced tribals inside the industrial zones, who were forced to live in slums on the outskirts or migrate to neighbouring states to work as labourers in terrible conditions. These tribals' migration to urban areas causes them emotional problems because they are unable to adjust to urban living and values.
4. **Health and Nutrition Issue:** Driven by economic backwardness and insecure livelihood, tribals face health issues such as disease prevalence including malaria, cholera, tuberculosis, diarrhoea, and jaundice, malnutrition problems such as iron deficiency and anaemia, high infant mortality rates, low levels of life expectancy, and so on.

5. **Gender Issues:** Women's position has been impacted by the degradation of the natural environment, particularly through the deforestation and a rapidly shrinking resource base. The opening of tribal belts to mining, industries, and commercialization exposed tribal men and women to the ruthless practices of the market economy, leading to consumerism and women's commoditization.
6. **Identity Erosion:** Traditional tribal institutions and laws are increasingly clashing with modern institutions, raising concerns among tribals about safeguarding their identity. Another source of concern is the extinction of tribal dialects and languages, which indicates a loss of tribal identity in some areas.

E-government and Tribal Development

E-government is not simply about putting forms and services online. It can provide the opportunity to rethink how the government offers, services and how it links them in a way that is tailored to the users' needs (Burn and Robins, 2003). E-government is one of the novel and most appealing applications of information and communication technologies (ICTs). It is defined as "the use of ICT in public administrations combined with organizational change and new skills in order to improve public services and democratic processes and strengthen support for public policies" (European Commission, 2003). It has been reported as an enabler to achieving better and more efficient public administration. E-government can act as a facilitator for equal access to information and empower people in all aspects of social arenas. In the absence of a free flow of information, there could be a tendency for some government officials to simply lie or be selective about the truth when caught in a situation in which they are expected to be accountable (Mutula, 2006: 447). If public organizations tend to equality, accountability, and transparency in their decision-making, e-government leads to good governance.

E-Government Initiative for Tribal Development

1. **Swasthya Portal:** Swasthya is a one-stop solution presenting the health and nutrition status of the tribal population of India. It is envisaged that the information available on Swasthya will provide insights to all stakeholders working with the tribal population of India in the areas of health and nutrition. Furthermore, it is hoped that this will result in evidence-based policymaking.
2. **DBT:** Its aim is to increase transparency, eliminate waste of funds, and allow for better monitoring of the schemes implemented by the government of India. In DBT, benefits or subsidies will be directly transferred to the bank accounts of the beneficiaries. The Public Finance Management System (PFMS) acts as the common platform for DBT. Every month, all state governments/UTs shall upload data regarding DBT Transactions on the portal.
3. **Tribal Digital Document Repository:** It is a unique digital repository of documents related to tribes in India, developed by NIC and content provided by the Ministry of Tribal Affairs, Government of India. Tribal Digital Document Repository provides Search and Browse options for Tribal Documents, allowing anyone to easily search and browse for the information they require. It provides the facility of a refined search, so everyone can easily find their relevant documents.
4. **1000 Spring Initiative:** The Spring Water Atlas is a repository of information on springs in the form of science behind the springs, spring sheds and springs cape. The GIS enabled Online inventory of springs will help in mapping of springs, analysing their health status, quality of water, discharge capacity and other physical, chemical and biological properties. The portal will strengthen various aspects of spring's management to address water scarcity in India.

5. **National Tribal Migration Support Portal:** It is a digital data solution that collects information about migrant workers. The information will be organised into four categories: demographic profile, livelihood, skill mapping, and migration pattern. The migration data will be available electronically and visible *via* dashboards at the village, block, district, state, and national levels for various tiers of government authorities.

Expected Outcome of the National Tribal Migration Support Portal

- Promoting local livelihood based on database-promoting Aatmanirbhar Bharat.
- Tailor-made programme to support migrating families in targeted manner backed up by data Formulation of suitable strategies and policy decision for making the existing schemes more effective and beneficiary friendly.
- Immediate support for tribal and other migrant workers in cities for safe and productive migration.

GIS-Enabled Entitlement Tracking System

The Union and State Governments of India have implemented a variety of social welfare programmes to assist the poor in particular. Unfortunately, these initiatives do not always reach the rural communities for which they are intended, resulting in biased or inefficient use of government funds. One major cause of this critical gap is a widespread lack of awareness about entitlements, which implies that most benefits are not received by rural communities in India.

The GIS Enabled Entitlement Tracking System (GEET) is a collaboration between the Ministry of Rural Development (MoRD), the United Nations Development Programme (UNDP), and the Foundation for Ecological Security (FES) to improve the reach, response, and review of social security scheme implementation. The GEET project aims to provide a single platform that assists rural communities in gaining access to various government schemes and programmes for which they are eligible. This system will also aid state, district, and government officials in monitoring access to entitlements and services and tracking progress. Thereby enabling communities claim their entitlements.

Adivasi Grants Management System (ADIGRAMS) Portal

It will serve as a single database for the Ministry of Tribal Affairs and the State Tribal Development/Welfare Department to access, interact with, and analyse current scheme information. Information on the physical and financial state of affairs, as well as advancement. Officials/stakeholders at the central, state, district, block, and village levels will be able to access, monitor, and measure performance in real time and make informed decisions using the site. The platform will also totally digitise the process of submitting and approving proposals under various MoTA schemes. This portal covers the following schemes of MoTA:

- Grants under Article 275(1) of the Constitution of India.
- Special Central Assistance (SCA) to Tribal Sub-Scheme (TSS).
- Scheme for Development of Particularly Vulnerable Tribal Groups (PVTGs).
- Institutional Support for Development and Marketing of Tribal Produce.
- Minimum Support Price (MSP) Mechanism for Minor Forest Produce (MFP) Marketing and Development of MFP Value Chain (MSP for MFPs).

GOAL

Education is the key intervention that will open doors to a better world. Going Online As Leaders (GOAL) is a digital literacy and mentorship initiative that lies at the foundation of this motto. Driven to empower and enable India's tribal youth, the key is to identify, mobilize, and connect over 2500 renowned leaders from the industry, who can personally mentor 5000 youth from tribal communities across the country.

Challenges for E-government Strategies for Tribal Development

Following are the obstacles in implementation of e-Governance in India:

- **Language Diversity:** Because e-Government apps are written in English, the diversity of people in terms of language poses a significant problem for executing e-Government initiatives. Furthermore, the majority of individuals may not be able to understand English. As a result, the government faces a problem in developing e-Government apps that will be implemented across the country in many languages and that will be acceptable to users of every language.
- **Inadequate IT Literacy**: A large portion of the Indian population is illiterate, and those who are literate lack expertise in information technology (IT). The majority of Indians are unaware of how to use information technology. As a result, India's low level of IT literacy is a key impediment to the deployment of e-Government.
- **Recognition of Applications:** Getting citizens to recognise e-government services is another significant difficulty. It is a problem to make all residents aware of the services provided by e-government and to gain their trust in them, so that citizens are willing to embrace these services.
- **User-friendliness of Government Websites:** E-government application users are frequently non-expert users who may not be able to fully utilise the applications correctly. Such users require assistance in determining the best course of action for their purchases. That is why government websites must be created in a more user-friendly fashion; only then will they be accessible to non-expert users.
- **Lack of Integrated Services:** The majority of governance services provided by the state or the federal government are

not linked. Its main cause could be a lack of communication between various government departments. As a result, information held by one department has no or little value in the eyes of other government departments.

- **Geographical Issues:** Corporate networks rely on secure and reliable networks. Government networks must be established in all areas, including those that are unsuitable for human habitation. It is, however, extremely expensive to wire up all of the country's villages. As a result, e-Government systems must use wireless networks, such as existing cellular networks, to reach applications in remote areas, regardless of geographical constraints.
- **Local Language:** English has a very low level of acceptance in India. The applications for e-governance are written in English. That is why e-Government projects are not successful. Thus e-governance applications must be written in the people's native language so that they can use and get benefit from them.
- **Interoperability:** The ability of systems and organizations of varying qualities to work together is referred to as interoperability. This feature must be present in e-Government applications so that new and existing applications can be implemented concurrently.
- **Scale of Applications:** E-Governance projects must be designed to scale from the start. Because e-Government is supposed to affect every citizen in the country, e-Government applications must be large enough to interface with every citizen.
- **Privacy and Security:** The privacy and security of an individual's personal data that he or she supplies to get government services is a major barrier to E-Government implementation. When e-government initiatives are implemented, some effective steps must be made to protect people's sensitive personal information. The growth of e-Government initiatives that contain personal

information such as income, medical history, and so on may be hampered by a lack of security standards.

- **Political Instability:** Political obstacles are caused by a lack of democratic engagement. Due to political conditions, the government faces challenges in implementing and using e-government services.

Conclusion

Governments worldwide are faced with the challenge of transformation and the necessity to reinvent government processes in order to deliver efficient and cost-effective services, information, and knowledge using information and communication technology. E-Government was catalysed and led by the advancement of information and communication technologies. The goal of e-government is to change the way the government interacts with the people it governs. The procedure is neither quick nor easy. The success of e-government requires fundamentally changing how the government works and how citizens perceive government assistance. Governments have different strategies to build e-government. Some have created comprehensive long-term plans. Others have opted to identify just a few key areas as the focus of early projects. In all cases, however, the tribals identified as most successful have begun with smaller projects in phases on which to build a structure. Research suggests e-governance has a lot of potential for bringing the government closer to tribal people by improving the speed and efficiency of their interactions. There are various obstacles that must be removed to realise its full potential. So, good e-governance must be based on:

- informed participation of the public in the governance processes;
- transparency;
- accountability;
- free speech;
- capability development; and
- IT and infrastructure development.

References

D.N. Gupta (2007). *Strategic Management for E-Governance*, http://www.iceg.net/2007/books/1/10-389.pdf.

http://frwebgate.access.gpo.gov/cgibin/getdoc.cgi?dbname=107_cong_public_laws&docid=f:publ347.107.pdf

http://klesnc.org/wp-content/uploads/2020/08/MRP-on-Overcoming-the-Societal-Challenges-in-impleme

http://meity.gov.in/divisions/national-e-governance-plan

http://www.ijstm.com/images/short_pdf/1487864238_P678-684.pdf

https://darpg.gov.in/sites/default/files/promoting_egov11.pdf

https://dbttribal.gov.in/

https://dl.acm.org/doi/10.1145/1509096.1509121

https://dl.acm.org/doi/10.1145/1509096.1509149

https://geet-undp.com

https://goal.tribal.gov.in

https://niti.gov.in/planningcommission.gov.in/docs/reports/sereport/ser/stdy_tribal.pdf

https://pib.gov.in/PressReleaseIframePage.aspx?PRID=15149.

https://pib.gov.in/PressReleasePage.aspx?PRID=1657743

https://repository.tribal.gov.in/

https://shramshakti.tribal.gov.in/Home.aspx

https://swasthya.tribal.gov.in/home

https://thespringsportal.org

https://tribal.nic.in/downloads/Statistics/OtherReport/DevelopmentChallengesinExtremistAffectedAreas.pdf

https://www.firstpost.com/tech/news-analysis/narendra-modi-reiterates-commitment-to-digital-india-says-govt-using-mobile-power-to-empower-indians-4224057.html

https://www.ijser.org/researchpaper/Barriers-to-e-Government-in-India.pdf

https://www.yourarticlelibrary.com/tribes/six-main-problems-faced-by-the-indian-tribes/42401

IJARCET-VOL-2-ISSUE-3-1196-1199_1.pdf (egovstandards.gov.in)

M.A.S. Rajan (2003). "Information Technology for the Villages and the Digital Divide". *Indian Journal of Public Administration.* Indian Institute of Public Administration (MPA). New Delhi. Vol. XIX, No 1, January-March, pp. 1-5.

Subash Bhatnagar (2004). *E-Government: From Vision to Implementation*, Sage Publications.

Syamal K. Ghosh and Rajanish Dass (2004), "Towards a Framework for E-governance in India", *Toward E-Government: Management Challenges.*

M.P. Gupta (Ed), Tata McGraw Hill Publishing Company Limited. New Delhi, pp. 247-255.

Wikipedia contributors. (2020, December 19). E-governance. In Wikipedia, The Free Encyclopedia. Retrieved 10:54, November 15, 2021.

12

PESA and Self-Governance in Fifth Scheduled Areas

Role of Governor

Nayakara Veeresha

Introduction

The indigenous communities all over the world are experiencing various forms of alienation. Among all, alienation of rights over land, forest and other natural resources is the most serious one. The evolution of 'modern nation-state' has usurpated territorial autonomy and traditional rights of indigenous peoples. India got Independence in 1947 and established Parliamentary Democracy in 1950. Indigenous people of India are known as Adivasis meaning the 'first inhabitants' with official name of 'Scheduled Tribe'. Most of them are concentrated in Central, Eastern and North-east regions. These regions are witnessing a variety of ethnic, socio-political conflicts. Adivasis are one of the few sections of society in India who do not shy away to rebel against the authority in power whenever their rights are violated and felt threatened to their culture and self-governance.

The continuum of various adivasis insurrections has a long history of 180 years staring from 1766 to 1945.

In order to contain the adivasis insurrections in different parts of the country, the colonial government has enacted legislations such as 'Laws Local Extent Act, 1874' and 'Scheduled Districts Acts of 1874'. The objective of these laws is of twofold—(i) to provide a stake for the local governments in administering these areas and (ii) to govern the scheduled districts in a non-regulatory mode. After this, the Government of India Act, 1919 classified the adivasi areas into 'wholly excluded areas' and 'areas with modified exclusion'. The terminology has got changed in the Government of India Act of 1935 with the names of 'excluded areas' and 'partially excluded areas'. In post-Independence period these are subsequently added in the Constitution in the form of Fifth Schedule (for partially excluded areas) and Sixth Schedule (for excluded areas). Andhra Pradesh, Chhattisgarh, Gujarat, Himachal Pradesh, Jharkhand, Madhya Pradesh, Maharashtra, Odisha, Rajasthan and Telangana states have FSAs. Except Gujarat, Himachal Pradesh and Rajasthan, the remaining states are experiencing insurrection. Among these 10 states, Chhattisgarh, Jharkhand and Odisha are 'worst affected' states by the insurrection. The socio-economic and political alienation of adivasis has produced discontent towards the current governance system and legitimacy crises of the States in India which is manifested in the form of Naxalism.

Context

Naxalism[1] in India is an armed political struggle. The roots of insurrection can go back to the agrarian uprisings in Telangana, Tebhaga (1946), Naxalbari (1967) regions of erstwhile Princely State of Hyderabad and West Bengal. The issues concerning the political insurrection in Central and Eastern India are multi-dimensional in nature. To illustrate, some of them are the policies towards tribal development, land acquisition in Scheduled Areas, rights over the natural resources such as minor forest produces, mineral deposits and other forest products, agrarian transformation, governance conflict, socio-economic and political exclusion of the disadvantaged sections of the society, needs of youth (education and employment), poverty, role of political ideology and the role of Indian State in reproducing structural violence in the countryside.

According to the Ministry of Home Affairs, Government of India, Bihar, Chhattisgarh, Jharkhand and Odisha States are severely affected by the Left-Wing Extremism.[2] The dominant discourses on Maoism/Naxalism/Left-Wing Extremism phenomenon attributes largely socio-economic and poverty factors responsible for the insurrection. It is not deniable that the areas of insurrection show poor socio-economic conditions, high poverty and backwardness; however, it is also important to analyse the evolution and functioning of modern State institutions such as Bureaucracy, Police, Judiciary, and Legislature in areas of insurrection. For example, it is observed that "the police outpost has always been considered by the tribals as an alien element. The behaviour of the other armed forces is not exemplary by any standard and they are being considered as less desirable elements than the district police forces (Government of India, 1987: 159)". Very few studies have made an attempt to understand the role of state, inquiring issues of governance, specifically adivasi's engagement in Gram Sabha as envisioned in PESA which recognises the right to self-governance of adivasis. Other governance aspects such as lack of effective democratic representation of adivasis issues in the Legislative Assembly, Parliament by elected representatives, inadequate devolution of powers to the Local Government Institutions, delay in the Justice system are not adequately dealt by the existing studies. One of the important aspects of governance which have not dealt adequately is the role of Governors and President in ensuring peace and good governance in Scheduled Areas.

Left-Wing Extremism is an official connotation used by the Ministry of Home Affairs, GoI to describe the phenomenon of insurrection. It must be noted that though the term 'Naxalism' is the popularly used term in Indian context, we can see a change in the nomenclature in policy documents of Government of India to explain the insurrectionary situation with the changing times. Other widely used terms for the insurrection ongoing in Central and Eastern States are Maoism/Extremism/Revolution etc.

Research Objective and Questions

The main purpose of this chapter is to explore the status of governance with particular reference to the role of governor in establishing peace and good government in Fifth Scheduled Areas (hereafter FSAs). It critically analyses the relationship between governance and insurrection. While flagging of some crucial issues of governance we specifically try to find out the plausible answers to the following research questions, is there any conflict between the State-led governance and Self-governance systems of adivasis in Fifth Scheduled Areas? To what extent the Governor has performed the constitutional role of ensuring peace and governance in Fifth Scheduled Areas of the State to contain the insurrection and land related conflicts in rural and adivasi areas.

Data Sources and Methodology

The data was mainly drawn from the critical analysis of the Annual Governor's Reports on the Administration of Scheduled Areas. Every year Governor of respective State belonging to FSAs have to submit annual report on the administration to the President of India as per the Article 244(1) of the Constitution of India. These data sets were primarily accessed through the Centre for Policy Research, New Delhi. Other sources of data and information are the annual budget speeches made by the Governors of FSAs States on the state of affairs. The year 2006 have been considered as reference period due to the following developments:

- Creation of a separate division within the Ministry of Home Affairs known as Naxal Management Division with an objective of tackling "the naxalite menace from both security and development angles (Government of India, 2007: 3)".
- Tabulation of the "Status of the Naxal Problem" by the then Union Home Minister Shivarj Patil in the Parliament.

- Enactment of "The Scheduled Tribes and Other Traditional Forest Dwellers (Recognition of Forest Rights) Bill, 2006".

The above developments indicate a change in perception of the Government of India towards dealing with Naxalism. "Naxalism is not merely a law-and-order problem; it has deep socio-economic dimensions (*ibid.*: 24)". This data has been corroborated by the preliminary observations of the author in Andhra Pradesh, Chhattisgarh and Telangana States facing insurrectionary challenge in severe form. The analysis and interpretation of data has been done using 'discourse analysis' and 'document analysis' techniques.

Fifth Scheduled Areas: An Overview of Article 244(1)

In India, 640 districts are present according to the Census of India, 2011. The FSAs are extended in 108 districts in ten States. It means that one by sixth of the districts come under the purview of the Fifth Schedule to the Constitution. The Fifth Schedule is popularly known as 'Constitution within the Constitution' as it lays an alternative scheme of governance within the Constitution by providing special provisions to administer the Scheduled Areas with more powers vested in the office of Governor than that of the State. The Fifth Schedule containing the 'Provisions as to the Administration and Control of Scheduled Areas and Scheduled Tribes' has been added to the Constitution following the motion moved by Ambedkar on 5th September, 1949. These provisions have great value in uplifting of Adivasis from all forms of social exploitation and injustice leading to their empowerment. Table 12.1, provides the notified list of States and districts of FSA.

Table 12.1: Notified List of Fifth Scheduled Areas

Andhra Pradesh (5)	Chhattisgarh (19)	Gujarat (11)	Himachal Pradesh (3)	Jharkhand (16)
Madhya Pradesh (20)	Maharashtra (12)	Odisha (13)	Rajasthan (5)	Telangana (4)

Source: Ministry of Panchayati Raj, Government of India.

The FSAs are governed by the Provisions of (Extension to Scheduled Areas) of Panchayats Act, 1996 popularly known as PESA. Article 244(1) of the Constitution provides special administrative arrangements to govern FSAs. One of the important provisions is that any law either passed by State or Union Government does not automatically apply to these areas unless the law was notified by the Governor of the concerned State as per the sub-clause 5(1) of the Article 244(1). It also specifies that "the Governor may make regulations for the peace and good government of any area in a State which is for the time being a Scheduled Area". Particularly, the Governor may make regulations to (a) prohibit or restrict the transfer of land by or among members of the Scheduled Tribes in such area; (b) regulate the allotment of land to members of the Scheduled Tribes in such area, and (c) regulate the carrying on of business as money-lender by persons who lend money to members of the Scheduled Tribes in such area.

Role of Governor in FSAs

Governors have accorded special responsibilities in ensuring peace and good government in Scheduled Areas. This provision is a continuation from the Government of India Act, 1935. With some modifications it was adopted by the Government of India in 1950. Article 244(1) of the Constitution provides special provisions to administer the Fifth Scheduled Areas. It is also the responsibility of the Governor to send Annual Reports to the President of India regarding the administration of Scheduled Areas in the State. Sections 5(1 to 4) accords special legislative powers to the Governor to oversee the applicability of any State or Union law to the Scheduled Areas. Section 5(2) of sub-clause (a, b, and c) provides provisions with specific reference to the land regulation and the allotment of land in Scheduled Areas. The following table provides the status of annual governor's report sent to the President from 2009 onwards especially the states facing the challenge to insurrection.

Table 12.2: Status of Annual Governor's Report in FSAs

Sl. No.	States	Governor's Reports received for the years						
		2009-10	2010-11	2011-12	2012-13	2013-14	2014-15	2015-16
1	Andhra Pradesh	R	R	A	A	A	A	A
2	Chhattisgarh	R	R	R	R	R	R	R
3	Jharkhand	R	R	R	R	A	A	A
4	Madhya Pradesh	R	R	R	R	R	A	A
5	Maharashtra	R	R	R	R	R	R	A
6	Telangana	NA	NA	NA	NA	NA	A	A

Source: Ministry of Tribal Affairs, GoI (2016-17) Abbreviations: R: Received; A: Awaited and Not Applicable.

FSAs are extended in ten States. However, in Table 12.2 we have considered the states only where socio-political conflict is going on between the State and insurgents. To understand the factors responsible for insurrection it is necessary to understand the functioning of State-led governance machinery. From Table 12.2 it is clear that except Chhattisgarh and Maharashtra, other States have not shown adequate interest and willingness to send annual Governor's report to the President of India.

A close reading of the Annual reports of the Governor 2008-09, 2009-10 Chhattisgarh State reveal that the reports have not dealt with issues concerning adivasis unrest, political violence and extremism in the State. Curiously, the reports mentioned the State Surrender policy for the Naxalites. The reports are only indicative of administrative activities of each department. From the reports we can infer that the reports have prepared just as documentation and not as a serious work by the respective State and Office of the Governor. The neglect of implementing the provisions of Fifth Schedule by the rulers in Post-Independence period has given rise to a variety of social and political upheavals in these areas with rampant land alienation.

Apart from this, the negligence of office of the Governors to supervise the implementation of laws such as Forest Rights Act, 2006 and PESA, 1996 concerned with the adivasis well-being is one of the critical factors that fuel the perception of deprivation of rights and injustice among the local communities. This has created a trust deficit among the adivasis towards the state institutions of governance. Hence, it is not surprising to note that most of the field functionaries of insurrection battle with the State come from the local adivasis and other disadvantaged sections of the community who are denied their legitimate rights of the Constitution. It is argued that the "Left-wing Extremism is a phenomenon largely confined to Fifth Scheduled Areas with an overwhelming population as its foot soldiers" (Sahoo, 2011:5).

According to the Ministry of Tribal Affairs the annual reports were submitted from 2009 onwards up to 2015-16. It must be noted that "Governors' reports rarely mention poor governance, insurgency or displacement" (Jitendra, 2013). It is interesting to note that Governors are well aware of the social and political unrest among the adivasis communities leading to the discontent and dissatisfaction towards the existing system of governance. To illustrate this point it is worth to draw from Lt. Gen. K.M. Seth, former Governor of Chhattisgarh and Tripura.

"The spread of Naxalism can be attributed to the inability of the State concerned to deliver the basic services and make the rural inhabitants, particularly, the tribal inhabitants the part of National Developmental process. This neglect provided the desired space to the naxalites who have been having roller coaster rides since 1967; the tribals were convinced that democratic form of Government is not suitable for them" (Amity, 2012).

In another instance Ved Marwah, former Governor of Jharkhand has observed that

> "As long as political and economic injustice exists and people have frustration against the system whether it is for political or economic demands or essential commodities, left wing extremism will remain. The

> only thing that has changed in the past 60 odd years is the strategy being used, the main goal is clear and they have come to the conclusion that a "so called parliamentary democracy" is an exploitative system and there is no hope of their getting justice from this political and administrative system (IPCS, 2012:14-15)".

A question arises here is that, why the Governors during their tenures in the office of Governor have failed to bring these realities to the President of India in their annual reports? Why Governors have not mentioned about poor governance, insurgency and social unrest in the Fifth Scheduled Areas while sending their annual reports to the President? What factors have hindered them not to deal and reflect about the critical issues of unrest in adivasis society?

A part of the answer may lie in the mode of appointment of Governor by the Governments in power at Union and State levels. The appointment of Governors is only by nomination and not through electoral system. In one way the indirect method of appointing Governors by the Union Government have a lot of space to exercise a strong influence on the special powers accorded under Article 244(1) in administering the FSAs. The political appointment of Governors has captured the executive powers of the office of Governors in the governance of adivasi areas. These are critical insights on how the constitutional authorities of the State are neglecting the role towards ensuring the good governance in Fifth Scheduled Areas.

Another factor is the usurpation of the executive authority in administering the Scheduled Areas by the respective State Governments. The State Governments are reluctant to devolve the powers to the office of the Governor. It is not wise to critique only the office of Governor for this state of affairs in adivasi areas. The State is also equally held responsible as it has not provided separate infrastructure, personnel and financial resources to discharge the functions by the Governor in accordance with the Article 244(1).

In this context, the office of the Governor of Maharashtra and the State has taken initiative to establish 'Tribal Cell' within the Governor's office in 2013. This shows that how slow we are in recognising the needs of governance in Scheduled Areas. Why does it took 65 years just to acknowledge and recognise the need for a separate administrative cell to assist the office of Governor in discharging the duties and to administer FSAs as per the Constitutional provisions. We as a country is yet to frame a national policy for adivasis with whom the knowledge of self-governance and sustainable development is preserved for a long period till 1991. Despite bearing the burden of national development cause the adivasis are one of the most vulnerable and exploited communities in the name of development and modernity.

The Panchsheel policy framework formulated by Jawaharlal Nehru, the first Prime Minister of India along with Verrier Elwin during the beginning of Independence has lost its primacy over the years. Developments such as excessive focus on economic growth, industrialisation, mining extractive policies, forceful land acquisitions for the development projects, agrarian changes, and exploitative forest policies have given rise to unrest, discontent in adivasis society. All these policies were implemented by the constitutional scheme of governance and democracy the adivasis communities are not in a position to trust the existing governance machinery. Ascertaining these facts, it was observed that:

> "It is necessary to trace the history of tribal dispossession over the last 150 years. The impact of the forest laws was tragic for self-governing, self-respecting tribal communities. I personally believe that whenever legislations or policies impact tribals unfavourably in Scheduled Areas, it becomes imperative on the institution of Governor to step in for the welfare of tribal communities" (Government of India, 2017: 36-37).

It is heartening to note that these observations has made by Vidyasagar Rao, Governor of Maharashtra and Tamil Nadu during his address in a national seminar. This is the positive side of the office of Governor taking keen interest in adivasi issues and trying to fulfil the constitutional responsibilities. On the other side there are attempts to undermine the executive powers of the office of Governor.

In Chhattisgarh, "the Chief Minister has made the *Ex-Officio* Chairman of Tribes Advisory Council (TAC)" (Government of India, 2012: 249). It is questionable that how Governor can appoint a Chief Minister as the *Ex-Officio* Chairman of Tribes Advisory Council. Though the Governor has the discretionary powers to elect the Chairman of the Tribes Advisory Council it is very important to elect such a person who have knowledge about the adivasis and expertise in the matters of local governance. This tells about the real intent and the reluctance of the State government to devolve the necessary powers to the Tribes Advisory Council to keep the decision-making powers with the State in the matters of well-being of adivasis. The changes in the mode of governance in post Independent India and the continued colonial policies of adivasis well-being transformed the lives of adivasis from self-sufficient and self-governing communities into the exclusive dependent on the State for their survival and welfare.

Why does the office of Governor have failed to prevent the land alienation, development induced displacement, exploitation of adivasis from local traders and inclination of adivasis towards radical politics? The answer can be given best as follows stated by the Sub-Committee in its interim report on 'The Excluded and Partially Excluded Areas (Other than Assam)' chaired by A.V. Thakkar in 1947. With regard to Partially Excluded Areas (Fifth Scheduled Areas in current terminology) the committee observed that,

> "The greatest weakness of the scheme of partial exclusion is perhaps the fact that it left areas weakly or only nominally represented in the legislature without any special financial provisions. Whatever the reasons

> maybe, the conclusion to be drawn from the state of affairs noticed by us is that partial exclusion or exclusion has been of very little practical value" (Rao et.al., 1967: 746).

It is beyond the scope of this chapter to enquire about the adoption of exclusion scheme in spite of the sub-committee apprehensions about the practicality of the scheme. However, it can be observed that definitely the Constitution of India may have altered the criteria to administer the tribal areas instead of following the colonial framework of governance. The remarks of the sub-committee are valid even today. To illustrate, for the whole of Bastar (bigger than smaller States of the country) have only one Member of Parliament. In public offices also adivasis have poor representation. Table 12.3 gives a glimpse of the representation of adivasis in comparison to Scheduled Castes.

Table 12.3: Representation of SC/ST in Public Offices

Level	Total	SC		ST	
		Number	Per cent	Number	Per cent
Secretary	72	4	5.55	2	2.78
Special Secretary	19	1	5.26	1	5.26
Additional Secretary	60	1	1.67	2	3.33
Joint Secretary	280	22	7.86	7	2.50

Source: Government of India (2014).

The inadequate representation of adivasis in legislative bodies (Parliament, Assemblies) and public offices is one of the main reasons for the unrest in FSAs. It is observed that "as a result of this insufficient representation, the problems of these areas do not receive the attention to which their size and importance entitle them" (*ibid.*: 748).

Policy Considerations

The above analysis indicates that the role and performance of Governor's office in fulfilling the Constitutional obligations of

Article 244(1) is very poor. To strengthen the Governor's position and to make the office of Governor effective in administering the Scheduled Areas the following prescriptions may be considered by the policy-makers:

- Providing necessary infrastructure and personnel to the office of Governor to discharge the functions as obligated under the Article 244(1).
- Empowering Governor's office with financial powers and not just legislative provisions.
- Institute provision in the Constitution for the non-intervention of political elites in the duties of Governor.
- Revisiting the colonial scheme of governance for FSAs.
- Tribal Cell as established by the Maharashtra Governor's office may be replicated wherever applicable in other States.
- Creating necessary checks and balances for the States not to interfere with the Governor's duty in administering the FSAs.

Concluding Observations

The office of Governor has failed in fulfilling the Constitutional responsibility of ensuring the peace and good governance in Fifth Scheduled Areas. All the States having more adivasis population need to change the functional role of Governors. The States have to show sufficient will and intent to transform the life of adivasis by harmonizing the laws related to adivasi's well-being. This sets the tone for the development of adivasis and their involvement in governance. These steps are necessary to reduce the inclination of adivasis particularly youth and other socio-politically alienated social groups towards the radical political ideologies. The security or military approach to contain the insurrection is not sufficient and further it escalates the violence not only between the insurgents and state and also between the different adivasis communities.

The rekindling of local governance through the office of Governor is one of the potential instruments to alter the lives of adivasis. The Governors have to exercise their discretionary and legitimate authority to bring positive developments in the lives of adivasis communities. It is high time for the Governor's office to effectively participate in the national building process by enabling proper implementation of the progressive laws enacted for the well-being of adivasis. This will help in reducing the 'trust deficit' among the adivasis communities and the State governments in the areas of insurrection.

Acknowledgement and Funding

The arguments made in this chapter are part of the ongoing doctoral dissertation work of the author. The research is being carried out at the Institute for Social and Economic Change (ISEC), Bengaluru with the financial support of Prof. V.K.R.V. Rao Fellowship in association with Indian Council for Social Science Research (ICSSR). I am grateful to my Supervisor Prof. N. Sivanna for his valuable guidance and support. I would like to express my sincere thanks to the Doctoral Committee members, Panel of Experts in particularly late Prof. B.S. Bhargava for their valuable comments and suggestions during the research progress from time to time. My special thanks to Dr. V. Anil Kumar for his academic inputs.

Note

1. The term 'Naxalism' has originated from the Naxalbari village in the Siliguri subdivision of Darjeeling district of West Bengal State. The village Naxalbari is one of the villages (Naxalbari, Khoribari and Phansidewa) where violent agrarian uprisings took place in 1967. From then onwards the term Naxalism has been in usage to describe the insurgents who are motivated and guided by the political ideologies of Marx-Lenin-Mao to capture the political power through armed struggle. In this chapter the term insurrection has been used to describe the 'Naxalism' phenomenon which is a loosely called term. The term insurgents in this paper means Naxalite or Maoist or Left-wing Extremist as described in the dominant discourses on Naxalism/Maoism. Indian State during post Independent period especially in post economic reforms period have widened the socio-economic inequalities. These have given rise to numerous land related conflicts. Now the conflict in the States of Central and Eastern region has developed to an extent of largest "internal security threat" that the

country is facing as described by the former Prime Minister of India Manmohan Singh in 2010.

References

Government of India (1987). Report of the Commissioner for Scheduled Castes and Scheduled Tribes—Twenty Eighth Report, New Delhi: National Commission for Scheduled Castes and Scheduled Tribes.

Government of India (2012) *Special Report on Good Governance for Tribal Development and Administration*, New Delhi: National Commission for Scheduled Tribes.

Government of India (2014). *Lok Sabha Unstarred Question* No. 549, New Delhi: Ministry of Personnel, Public Grievances and Pensions.

Government of India (2017). *Annual Report 2016-17*. New Delhi: Ministry of Tribal Affairs.

Government of India (2017). SRSC Seminar Proceedings of 'Governance, Resources and Livelihoods of Adivasis in India: Implementation of PESA and FRA' held on 18-19 November, 2016, organized by the National Institute of Rural Development & Panchayati Raj (NIRD & PR) under the auspices of S.R. Sankaran Chair (Rural Labour), Hyderabad: Ministry of Rural Development.

Government of India, New Delhi: Ministry of Panchayati Raj. http://pesadarpan.gov.in/en_US/state-profiles

Government of India. (2007). *Annual Report 2006-07*. New Delhi: Ministry of Home Affairs.

http://www.amity.edu/events/eventdetails.asp?id=2220

IPCS (2012). *Conference Report* No. 38, The Naxal Problem: Understanding the Issues, Challenges and Alternative Approaches, New Delhi: Institute of Peace and Conflict Studies.

Jitendra (2013), "Governors in the dock", Down to Earth, 2013 can be accessible at http://www.downtoearth.org.in/news/governors-in-the-dock-40701 (last accessed on 07.10.2014).

Sahoo, N. (2011), "Dealing with Maoist Threats: The Development and Governance Conundrum", *ICSSR Journal of Abstracts and Reviews - Political Science*, Vol. *37*(2):1-25.

Shiva, R. *et al* (1967). *The Framing of India's Constitution: Select Documents*, Vol. III, for The Indian Institute of Public Administration, New Delhi: Metropolitan Publishers.

13

How PESA had Failed in Ensuring "Mava Nate Mava Raj (Our Village Our Rule)"?

Sandeep Tripathi and *Pushpender Yadav*

Introduction

With the realization of the limitation rather the failure of traditional approach of centralized planning and top-down approach to economic development of our country, several new alternatives came to be emphasized and focused on people-centric development, decentralized governance and participatory approach to development to get rid of the ills of under-development and poverty that our country has been confronted with all these years (Mohapatra, 2015: 156). Due to this developmental approach, public participation in the political system acquired necessity and focus shifted towards the inclusive political process where previously excluded sections of society like Tribals and other Indigenous groups, must be engaged, can raise the voice in subject matters affecting them and can participate in the mainstream line of economic and social development. In 1979, at World Conference on Agrarian Reform and Rural Development (WCARRD), world had united over the interpretation of public participation and introduced a strong framework which later on fostered the activities and thinking of many governments and developmental agencies.

Also researches on decentralisation have found that a decentralisation in governance and better implementation of public policies has proportional relation (Bardhan & Dilip Mookherjee, 2006; Muller, 2012; Oxhorn, Tulchin, & Selee, 2004). "Decentralisation in governance is expected to encourage constructive public engagement, improve effective transparency, and provide more accountability. By bringing government close to the public, decentralised governance is expected to suit their requirement and preferment" (Islam & Vyas, 2003). "Decentralised governance, from the national to rural levels, regions, districts, towns, municipalities, local settlements, and communities, is an essential prerequisite for inclusive governance because it allows people to contribute much directly in the decision-making process and strengthen communities who were previously neglected from the governing process" (Monditoka, 2010).

In context of India, the conception of public participation has been well enshrined in our Constitution. Article 40, which is related to the "Directive Principles of State Policy" states the constitution of Gram Panchayat by the state and call upon the state to endow these bodies with the function and power to allow them to act as a self-governing unit (Mohapatra, 2015). Hence, the Panchayati Raj System in India promoted as a decentralized system of governance holding all the participants in the development process. Following the global trend of people's participation India strengthen the local self-governance by conferring them constitutional status through 73rd Constitutional Amendment in 1992 and also added Part IX in Constitution which contains various provisions related to Gram Subhas and Gram Panchayats, their constitution, powers, functions and election. The main objective of this step was to empower the excluded societies left behind in the development journey by flowing power through the decentralising process by ensuring their participation in governance, making them determinants of their own destiny. Among all, the primitive segment of India's society adivasis are most excluded and sidelined in the process of development but Article 243-M prevents the states to apply provisions of that Panchayat and Local Self-Government laws in 'Scheduled and Tribal Areas' until Parliament formulates a special law with necessary modifications under the Fifth and Sixth Schedules of Constitution.

Tribal Scenario of India

As per the 2011 Census, in India, the Scheduled Tribe population is 10.4 crore individuals, accounting for 8.6 per cent of the overall population. The Constitution identifies 461 ethnic groups as STs, but as stated by one research, this number might rise to 635, implying that these figures are significantly undervalued (Stidsen & Dahl, 2006). More than two-third of total tribal population resides in the Chhattisgarh, Madhya Pradesh, Odisha, Rajasthan, Gujarat, Jharkhand and Maharashtra mostly concentrated in rural areas.

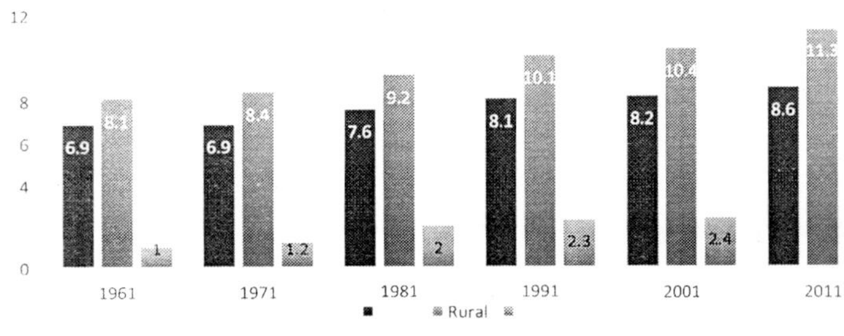

Fig. 13.1: Percentage of Scheduled Tribes in Overall Population

Source: 15th Census of India, 2011.

Scheduled Areas and PESA

Rectifying historical errors in attempt to attain substantive equity and distributive justice and governance mechanism which is found pertinent for the rest of the country, also necessary for development of adivasi communities. In this context, Indian

Parliament legislated "The Panchayats (Extension to Scheduled Areas) Act" (PESA) in 1996 to expand the Panchayati Raj System to the Scheduled areas. In Article 244(1), the words "Scheduled Areas" are defined as "such areas which is declare by the President of India as Scheduled Areas by the order in accordance with the Central Act." The predominance of tribal people, compactness and fair extent territory, impoverished standards of area, and significant discrepancy in economic conditions of the people are the criteria used to declare an area as a Scheduled Area (Monditoka, 2010: 8). These criteria did not define in the Constitution of India, but broadly built around the determinants accepted in declaring 'Excluded' and 'Partially Excluded Areas' under the Government of India Act, 1935, and defined in the Report of the Scheduled Areas and Scheduled Tribes Commission, 1961. Following consultation with state governments, the President issued the "Scheduled Areas (Part A States) Order, 1950", and the "Scheduled Areas (Part B States) Order, 1950", which defined the Scheduled Areas in the 10 States (Monditoka, 2010: 9).

The Spirit of PESA

In considering of candid demand of expanding the provisions of Part IX to the Scheduled Areas so as to ensure self-governance for tribal population considering with their customary law, social practices and religious traditions and conventional management of community resources, the Government of India appointed Bhuria Committee in 1994. On the basis of Bhuria Committee Report, 'The Panchayats (Extension to Scheduled Areas) Act' (PESA) was enacted in 1996 and came into force on December 24, 1996 with respect to Scheduled Areas under Fifth Schedule.

In PESA, Sections 4(a) and 4(d) capsulised the intrinsic soul of the Act, reacknowledge the superiority of conventional laws, traditional management for community resources and dispute resettlement. These sections are stated below:

4(a) "A legislation so states on Panchayats must be consistent with customary law, social and religious norms, and traditional community resource management techniques."

4(b) "Every Gram Sabha shall be responsible for safeguarding and preserving the people's traditions and customs, cultural identity, resources, and traditional conflict resolution methods." (Ministry of Tribal Affairs, February 2016: 25)

PESA instructs State acts in Scheduled Areas to be revised in a year to assure that Gram Sabha should be capable to protect and conserve the customs and culture of the tribals.

How PESA had Failed in Insuring Tribal Self-governance?

The PESA, which was created by the government to strengthen tribal populations residing in the Fifth Scheduled territories and was formerly widely regarded as one of the most effective pieces of tribal law, is celebrating its silver anniversary this year. However, ruling elites who were expected to put it in place and carry it out have given it the cold shoulder. "PESA is impotent since 40 per cent of the states under it have failed to create rules for its implementation, including Chhattisgarh, Jharkhand, Madhya Pradesh, and Odisha, who have yet to do so, and Gujarat managed the Fifth Scheduled Areas using the Panchayati Raj Act's rules." (Pandey, 2021). Pointing out the significance of the PESA Act, a former Commissioner for SC and ST, B.D. Sharma who also contributed in drafting PESA and also known as 'The Mahatma of Tribals' (Lapalikar, 2015) wrote to the President of India in 2010 and said, "PESA's provisions looked to be a saviour, aiming to correct previous injustices against the tribal people. It sparked unparalleled fervour among tribal peoples all around the country. It was interpreted as a return to their dignity and self-governance traditions, as expressed by 'Mava Nate Mava Raj' (Our Village Our Rule)" (Pandey, 2021). He travelled all over the country with translated copies of the PESA and enlightened the local tribal communities about its significance but in recent times he argued that if we look at the journey of the Act, the sparkle of PESA has faded away as the ruling class is not ready to follow the spirit of the Act (Mohapatra R., 2015). Major reasons for that fade away are as follows: Unsatisfied Status of Mandatory Provisions in Scheduled Area States.

Table 13.1: Provisions of PESA, 1996 and their status

Sl. No.	Components	Mandatory Provisions	Status
1.	Village's Definition	Sec. 4(b): "A village is made up of a habitation that make up a community and manage their matters according to local customs and traditions."	This definition is accepted by all states except Maharashtra, which is mute in this issue.
2.	Status and Functions of Gram Sabha	Sec. 4(d): "Gram Sabha, will be responsible for preserving and safeguarding the people's traditions and practices, as well as their cultural identity."	The Central Act is followed by all State Acts. However, when it comes to the customary manner of conflict settlement, Andhra Pradesh impose the restriction in accordance with existing law and Orissa further extended this restriction to Constitutional values and Human Rights principles.
3.	Constitution of Panchayat	In accordance with Part IX of the Constitution, panchayats shall be formed at the village level, including reservations for Scheduled Tribes.	In Himachal and Andhra Panchayat Act, Both Gram Panchayats and Mandal/ intermediate Panchayats have been granted elective seats and Chairpersons. It is not mentioned in Maharashtra Act.
4.	Land Acquisition for Development Programme and Relocation of Uprooted Peoples	Sec. 4(i): "Mandatory prior consultation with Gram Sabha or Panchayats"	Andhra Pradesh did not follow this and Gujarat delegated this authority to Taluka Panchayats, but there was no framework for state-level coordination of such initiatives. Also in Orissa, Gram Sabha and Panchayat have no role, power is delegated to Zila panchayat.

(*Contd.*)

Sl. No.	Components	Mandatory Provisions	Status
5.	Licence or Mining Lease for Minor Minerals	Sec. 4(k): "Prior consultation with Gram Sabha or Panchayat would be required."	In Andhra Pradesh, the Gram Panchayat takes precedence over the Gram Sabha. It is not mentioned in Gujarat. Himachal Pradesh has preserved its Gram Sabha primacy, however the phrase "must be made necessary" has been substituted with "shall be taken into account". Madhya Pradesh, no mention of it in the Act.
6.	Minor Forest Produce (MFP) Ownership	Sec. 4(m)(ii): "Panchayats at the proper level, as well as Gram Sabha with ownership powers"	All State Acts, like the Central Act, delegate this authority to Gram Panchayat or Sabha.
7.	Prevention & Restoration of Tribal Land Alienation	Sec. 4(m)(iii): "Panchayats at the proper level, as well as the Gram Sabha, should be given this authority."	The Amendment Acts in Gujarat, Himachal Pradesh, and Madhya Pradesh do not provide for this. In Madhya Pradesh, however, the Land Revenue Code of 1959 was revised to provide Gram Sabha power.
8.	Money Lending to The STs	Panchayats at the proper level, as well as the Gram Sabha, should be given this authority.	Madhya Pradesh Amendment Act does not talk about anything about this.

Source: Planning Commission, 2001, pp. 98-100.

Insufficient Subject Delegation to Panchayats in Scheduled Areas

Insufficient subject delegation to Panchayats in Scheduled Areas is a significant issue, revealing disparities in the implementation of the 11th Schedule (Article 243G) of the Indian Constitution across various PESA states. The 11th Schedule lists 29 subjects intended to be devolved to panchayats to ensure decentralised governance and local self-management. However, there is a pronounced inconsistency in how different states have operationalized this constitutional mandate (Tata Institute of Social Sciences, 2015-16).

Himachal Pradesh emerges as an exemplar, having delegated all 29 subjects to its panchayats, thus fully complying with the 11th Schedule. This comprehensive delegation enables panchayats in Himachal Pradesh to manage a broad spectrum of local affairs, including agriculture, land development, minor irrigation, animal husbandry, fisheries, rural housing, drinking water, education, and health services(Tata Institute of Social Sciences, 2015-16). Such extensive delegation is crucial for fostering holistic and sustainable local development.

Conversely, states such as Madhya Pradesh and Telangana have delegated only 14 subjects each. This limited delegation severely restricts the Panchayats' functional domain, confining their roles to basic sectors and excluding critical areas such as minor forest resources, non-traditional energy resources, and technical education. The restricted empowerment of panchayats in these states undermines their capacity to address comprehensive local needs and challenges.

Andhra Pradesh and Rajasthan, despite delegating 25 subjects, still fall short in crucial sectors like technical and vocational education and rural electricity distribution. These omissions hinder the panchayats' ability to advance local infrastructure and human resource development, both essential for economic growth and social well-being (Tata Institute of Social Sciences, 2015-16). Jharkhand and Chhattisgarh, with 18 and 20 subjects delegated, respectively, illustrate additional gaps in subject delegation. These states have not included significant areas such as community and farm forestry, non-traditional energy resources, and robust social welfare programs(Tata Institute of Social Sciences, 2015-16). Consequently, panchayats in these regions face constraints in managing environmental conservation and social welfare, which are critical for sustainable local development.

The observed insufficiencies in subject delegation not only contravene the objectives of the PESA Act but also impede the realisation of decentralised governance envisioned by the 11th Schedule. Panchayats, hindered by these limitations, struggle to implement local development projects effectively, manage natural resources, and deliver essential services. This governance deficit can result in slower socio-economic progress and exacerbate local issues.Addressing these discrepancies requires a more uniform and comprehensive transfer of subjects to panchayats across all PESA states. Ensuring full delegation would empower panchayats to function as genuine self-governing institutions, capable of implementing development initiatives tailored to the unique needs of their communities. Academically, this would align with the principles of decentralised governance and local empowerment, fostering inclusive and sustainable development in India's Scheduled Areas.

Land Alienation and Acquisition

Section 4(m)(iii) of PESA states that:

> "State Legislature shall ensure that the Panchayats at the appropriate level and the Gram Sabha are endowed specifically with to prevent alienation of land in the Scheduled Areas and to take appropriate action to restore any unlawfully alienated land of a Scheduled Tribe." (PESA, Act No. 40 of 1996)

Source of this section rooted in the Constitution of India, as paragraph 5(2)(a) of Fifth Schedule prohibits or restrict the transfer of land from tribal to non-tribal in Scheduled Area and gave the mandate to the Governor to ensure that by enacting regulations.

Table 13.2: Landholding by Size class

Sl. No.	Size Groups	Number of Holdings (in '000)							
		1980-81	**1985-86**	**1990-91**	**1995-96**	**2000-01**	**2005-06**	**2010-11**	**2015-16**
1	Marginal	2728	3161	3763	4376	4429	5118	6470	7127
2	Small	1551	1795	2087	2336	2411	2650	2877	2972
3	Semi-Medium	1405	1545	1694	1778	1653	1700	1787	1771
4	Medium	936	936	943	898	783	763	760	704
5	Large	234	212	183	135	128	112	111	95
	All Sizes	**6854**	**7648**	**8670**	**9523**	**9404**	**10343**	**12005**	**12669**

Source: Department of Agriculture, Co-Operation & Farmers Welfare, 2019, p.15.

However, these provisions have not been succeeded to fulfil the constitutional duty of assuring that tribal communities will preserve their control over their traditional recourses. As the Report of the Department of Land Resources, Ministry of Rural Development, Government of India, in July 2013, states that:

- There were 3.75 lakh cases of tribal land alienation filled, encompassing 8.55 lakh acres of land;
- From above, 1.62 lakh cases (43.2%) were decided in favour of tribals, covering a total area of 4.47 lakh acres which is 58.28%; and
- The courts rejected 1.55 lakh (41.1%) of the cases, encompassing 3.63 lakh acres, on various grounds. (Ministry of Tribal Affairs, February 2016).

The Twelfth Five Year Plan Document also acknowledged the fact in its Chapter 24 (Social Inclusion) that at least 55 per cent of all displaced people are from tribals and in states like Gujarat this rate is above 76 per cent, also only 29 per cent of the affected have been rehabilitated leaving behind 13.2 million peoples uprooted from their homelands. Additionally, the portion of ST households with small and marginal land holdings has been regularly moving upwards over the time (see Table 13.2) and also variation in operational holdings of ST communities is in negative numbers in maximum Fifth Scheduled States (see Table 13.3).

Table 13.3: Number and Area of operational holdings for STs (2015-16)

Sl. No.	State/UTs	2015-16		2010-11		Variation%	
		Number	Area	Number	Area	Number	Area
1.	Andhra Pradesh	12	64	16	92	-29.81	-30.31
2.	Chhattis-garh	95	543	104	599	-8.62	-9.33
3.	Madhya Pradesh	138	776	154	890	-10.65	-12.77
4.	Gujarat	51	288	50	286	0.86	0.84

(*Contd.*)

5.	Himachal Pradesh	1	5	1	5	-7.28	-6.69
6.	Jharkhand	66	376	67	385	-2.03	-2.23
7.	Odisha	18	96	21	122	-15.04	-21.69
8.	Telangana	13	66	18	98	-31.74	-32.94
9.	Karnataka	25	142	26	146	-3.55	-2.71

Source: Department of Agriculture, Co-Operation & Farmers Welfare, 2019, p.33.

PESA, 1996 was the first step towards the decentralisation in tribal area of Fifth Schedule. It warranted the several political, administrative and fiscal powers to Gram Sabha and Panchayats elected by local tribal societies, while aiming to conserve their traditional customs and community resource management methods. "It has therefore been billed the logical extension to Fifth Schedule" (Government of India, 2006, p. 84). "But a closer look at the law, and its implementation proves, it is really half-hearted decentralisation" (Faraz, Bose, & Ghusale, 2016). Instead of empowering tribal communities to make decisions for themselves, PESA just tells state governments to consult, engage, and receive recommendations, rather than placing them in the driver's seat to raise their voices and negotiate issues that affect their life, culture, and wellness. The process of implementation of PESA has been bleak and its dismal enactment has disseminated the message that 'Mava Raj' is the natural and constitutional rights of the tribal societies. "Due to this, a sense of denial has been engendered in the minds of tribals due to clear violation of this legislation, which forced people to make alliance and seek redress with what the state dubs as extremists" (Sharma, 2010). Thus, above discussion showed that government only enacted the Act never pushed to frame mandatory rules, did not take seriously to Gram Sabha, Insufficient subject devolution arbitrary land alienation failed the PESA from insuring 'Mava Nate Mava Raj'.

References

15th Census of India. Government of India (2011).

Bardhan, P. & Dilip Mookherjee. (2006). *Decentralization and Local Governance in Developing Countries: A Comparative Perspective.* Cambridge: MIT Press.

Department of Agriculture, Co-Operation & Farmers Welfare (2019). *Agriculture Census 2015-16.* New Delhi: Ministry of Agriculture & Farmers Welfare, Government of India.

Faraz, M.A., Bose, R., & Ghusale, S. (2016). *The Extent and Nature of Individual Tribal Land Alienation in Fifth Schedule States in India.* New Delhi: Indian Council for Social Science Research (ICSSR).

Government of India (2006). *Report of the working group on land relations for formulation of the 11th Plan.* New Delhi: Planning Commission.

Islam, M.N. & Vyas, A. (2003). Decentralised governance and development in India: A study on West Bengal (*Working Paper No. 141*). Bangalore: Institute of Social and Economic Change.

Lapalikar, V. (2015, December 28). *Mahatma of the Tribals.* Retrieved November 2021, from Indianexpress.com: https://indianexpress.com/article/opinion/columns/mahatma-of-the-tribals/

Ministry of Tribal Affairs. (February 2016). *Land and Governance Under the Fifth Schedule.* New Delhi: Ministry of Tribal Affairs, Government of India.

Mohapatra, B. (2015). "People-Centric Governance and PESA". In N. Tiwari, *Tribal Self-Governance: PESA and its Implication.* Rawat Publications.

Mohapatra, R. (2015, December 31). *The Flame of Forest Rages on.* Retrieved November 2021, from downtoearth.org.in: https://www.downtoearth.org.in/news/governance/the-flame-of-forest-rages-on-52167

Monditoka, K.A. (2010). *Decentralised Governance in Tribal India: Negotiating Space between the State, Community and Civil Society.* Newcastle upon Tyne: Cambridge Scholars.

Muller, R.D. (2012). *Decentralization, Local Governance, and Social Well-being.* London: Routledge.

Oxhorn, P., Tulchin, J.S. & Selee, A. (2004). *Decentralization, Democratic Governance, and Civil Society in Comparative Perspective: Africa, Asia, and Latin America.* Washington DC: Woodrow Wilson Center Press.

Pandey, K. (2021, March 4). *PESA: The Wait for Reforms on the Ground Continues even after 25 years.* Retrieved November 2021, from Mongabay.com: https://india.mongabay.com/2021/03/pesa-the-wait-for-reforms-on-the-ground-continues-even-after-25-years/

PESA, Act No. 40 of 1996. (1996, December 24th). Retrieved November 2021, from legislative.gov.in: https://legislative.gov.in/sites/default/files/A1996-40.pdf

Planning Commission (2001). *Report of the Task Force on Panchayati Raj Institutions* (PRIs). New Delhi: Planning Commission.

Sharma, B. (2010). *Unbroken History of Broken Promises: Indian State and the Tribal People*. New Delhi: Freedom Press and Sahyog Pustak Kuteer.

Stidsen, S., & Dahl, J. (2006). *The Indigenous World 2006*. Copenhagen: International Workgroup for Indigenous Affairs.

Tata Institute of Social Sciences. (2015-16). *Tata Institute of Social Sciences Devolution Study 2015-2016*. Retrieved November 2021, from Panchayat.gov.in: https://www.panchayat.gov.in/documents/448457/0/Devolution+of+Power+in+PESA+States+%281%29.pdf/966d8704-5036-ad62-cd77-1b8cb7fb72b7?t=1632828558340

14

Land Acquisition in India

Unfurling Panchayats (Extension to Scheduled Areas) Act, 1996 as a Saviour of Scheduled Areas

Shivani Tiwari and *Pushpender Yadav*

Introduction

India holds a unique distinction of being the world's largest constitutional democracy and one of its fastest-growing economy. This has been achieved through continuous efforts of the government and the people of the country. Land acquisition is one of the important activities in the development process (Yoshino, Paul, Sarma, & Lakhia, 2018). To achieve double-digit GDP growth rate, land is fundamental. Union and State Government in India exercise the power to acquire private land for the purpose of industrialization, development of infrastructure and to compensate the affected landowners for their rehabilitation and resettlement (GoI, n.d.). Land acquisition finds centre stage in terms of many controversies and public policy paralysis in India (Goswami, 2011).

India is an agrarian economy with farmers as its backbone. Agriculture with its allied sectors is one of the largest livelihood providers in India and contributes significantly to GDP (GoI, Agriculture, n.d.). Having great geographical diversity, India has a varied land use pattern with 46 per cent of its area in under agriculture and 22 per cent is forest cover. But with continuous degradation, we have lost almost 70 per cent of good quality agricultural land. Land degradation is affecting 3.2 billion people worldwide and ecosystem services like forest, grasslands, agriculture etc. worth $10.6 trillion are lost every year due to land degradation only (UNESCO, 2018). Land is already stressed so much acquisition is adding to the problems of locals. India has always provided special protections for her tribal and indigenous people by recognizing their distinctive cultural, social and economic identity from the mainstream Indian society (UN, n.d.). Even after having strict laws and special provisions in the constitution of society, land is central to the livelihood of tribal communities but also a mark of their identity (Mohanty, 2019). The Scheduled Areas consist of several heterogeneous tribal groups with a distinctive way of life.

The geographical isolation of these people is due to the fact that they live in forested and hilly areas, which is less accessible to the people living in plains (Gogoi, Goswami & Borah, 2009). Plains have a settled agricultural livelihood but people of Scheduled Areas are engaged in traditional occupations including shifting cultivation, collecting minor forest produce and hunting gathering. And land was the main source of their livelihood, thus people feel more connected to their land (Aditya, 2021). Due to this fragility of the rights of tribal people, the Constitution of India has provided for the protection of the same. Articles 241(1) and 244(2) of the Constitution has granted special status to tribes associated with their land. These areas are called as the Fifth Schedule and Sixth Schedule to the Constitution under which special provisions are mentioned.

The Fifth Schedule provides for the administration of areas where the population of STs is in minority, compared to the population of the rest of the state. These areas are in Andhra Pradesh, Chhattisgarh, Telangana, Odisha, Maharashtra, Rajasthan, Madhya Pradesh, Himachal Pradesh, Jharkhand and Gujarat. It confers special powers on the Governor of the state having

Scheduled Areas for the effective governance of Scheduled Areas (Singh, 2019).

For a long period of time the land laws used to be governed by archaic British laws. Till 2014, Land Acquisition Act of 1894 was in force which provided only a minimal monetary compensation linked with market value of the land. In 2013 a new Act came—The Right to Fair Compensation and Transparency in Land Acquisition, Rehabilitation Act, 2013 provided rehabilitation and resettlement. It replaced the Land Acquisition Act, 1894. But the Act of 2013 exempted 13 laws from its purview, so an ordinance was passed in 2014- The Right to Fair Compensation and Transparency in Land Acquisition, Rehabilitation and Resettlement (Amendment) Ordinance which brought compensation, rehabilitation and resettlement provisions of those 13 laws (such as the National Highways Act, 1956 and Railways Act, 1989) in consonance with the Right to Fair Compensation and Transparency in Land Acquisition, Rehabilitation and Resettlement Act, 2013 (India, 2015). After the adoption of the Constitution, the Parliament and State Legislatures have enacted various laws to safeguard the rights of tribes. These laws prohibit the transfer of land from STs to non-tribals. In the year 1996 Parliament enacted the Panchayat Extension to Scheduled Areas Act to give more powers to Scheduled Areas over their lands, in 2006 it enacted the Forest Rights Act to safeguard the rights of tribals and other forest dwellers. 47.1 per cent of the STs are living below the poverty line in rural areas whereas 28.8 per cent of STs are below poverty line in urban areas (Falak, 2018). Despite there being a special constitutional provision in place for protection of the land rights, 9.4 per cent of the STs are landless (Wahi). Therefore, it is important to look upon the aspects of land acquisition which have bad consequences for tribes.

Objectives of the Study

1. To identify the problems of land acquisition in Scheduled Areas.

2. To examine the legal framework and different aspects of PESA, 1996.
3. To find out the effectiveness of PESA, 1996 in Scheduled Areas.
4. To suggest some measures to be taken to secure the land rights of tribals.

Research Methodology

Doctrinal and descriptive study:

1. The study was based on secondary data, so it has been collected from the various secondary sources such as websites, journals and other e-sources.
2. To explain the descriptive study, statistics were used.

Land Acquisition

Land is an important resource for most of the economic activities aimed at growth, in the world. The management of land resources is, therefore, considered as an important component of policymaking of a country. Even the World Bank has given heed to the distress of the tribals when in 1992 it forced to review its aided projects which face widespread criticism. The world institutions have stressed upon a proper rehabilitation policy and review of ecological concerns. The starting of development related projects could be traced during the times of Britishers, construction of first state owned Yamuna Canal system in 1789. Involuntary displacement became an issue of concern after the construction of Anicut Dam on Cauvery in 1863. Widespread criticism led to the enactment of Land Acquisition Act in 1894. Dams, industrial and mining projects, national parks, sanctuary and tourist places have displaced a lot of people. Proposals for large scale water resource management projects ignored displacement assessment and the costs of rehabilitation (Batabyal, 1999).

Table 14.1: Tribal Families Displaced due to Construction of Water Canals

	Resources in Madhya Pradesh	
Sl. No.	**Name of the project**	**No. of ST population displaced**
1.	Ban Sagar	32830
2.	Tawa	2618
3.	Indira Sagar	4405
4.	Upper Wainganga	1160
5.	Kojar	609
6.	Kodar	2479
7.	Mahi	7599
8.	Omkareshwar	776
9.	Dholawad Tank	1534
10.	Dejia Dewada	1390
11.	Bah	157
12.	Bariyarpur Left Bank Canal	900
13.	Mahan (Gulab Sagar)	1667
14.	Rajiv Gandhi	2598
15.	Rajghat (MP+UP)	5920
16.	Rampurakhurd Medium Project	760

Source: Lok Sabha Starred Question No. 198, dated, 22-8-2013.

United Nations defines internal displacement as—the person or group of persons who are forced to leave their habitual residence in order to avoid any armed conflict, situations of generalised violence, violation of human rights or natural or homemade disasters, who have not crossed international border. Indian investment in projects is huge and this has been possible due to acquisition of land, which causes massive displacement of people. Displacement due to development accounts for about 50 million people in over 50 years (Portal, n.d.). The government data itself says that a lot of tribals are displaced due to development projects. People in Schedule Areas continue to be the most vulnerable and impoverished section.

Table 14.2: Per centage distribution of agricultural and non-agricultural land holdings by STs for agricultural year July 2018-June 2019

Size class of land possessed(ha.)	Agricultural households	Non-agricultural households	Rural households
<0.01	0.3	29.2	11.1
0.01- 0.40	24.5	63.5	39.1
0.40- 1.00	44.2	4.5	29.3
1.01–2.00	21.3	2.6	14.3
2.01–4.00	7.9	0.2	5.0
4.01–10.00	1.6	0.0	1.0
10.00+	0.1	0.0	0.1

Source: 77th Round-NSS, Situation Assessment of Agricultural Households and Land and Holdings of Households in Rural India, 2019.

Land holdings among STs is very low, in the category of 2-10 ha., there are few households that show they are very poor. Land acquisition has claimed a lot from the livelihood of tribals. Scheduled Areas: The classification and distribution of tribes in the country was of less importance for Britishers as they were only concerned with the economic advantage of forests. Post-independence, there was a narrative in the policy making arena that "development through integration is the need of the hour." The Kalelkar Commission, 1995 classified the Scheduled Tribes and denotified (ex-criminal tribes) along with Scheduled Castes, women and other socially and economically and educationally backward classes. It also recommended identification of certain backward districts as Scheduled Areas. In the year 1959, Renuka Ray Committee on Social Welfare and Welfare of Backward Classes gave the same definition and recommended that welfare measures should help them evolve through their own social and cultural institutions. Dhebar Committee in 1960 established the following factors to be considered while declaration of any area as scheduled:

(a) preponderance of tribals in the population;
(b) the compactness and reasonable size of the area;

(c) underdeveloped nature of the area; and
(d) marked disparity in the economic standard of the people.

This Commission identified the isolation of tribes based on their geographic location. Later in 1993, Bhuria Commission came up with the idea of special provisions for Scheduled Areas. Article 241(1) of the Constitution, expression 'Scheduled Areas' mean such areas as the President may by order declare to be Scheduled Areas. Under this, the Governor is empowered to take actions regarding the transfer of land by or among the members of the Scheduled Tribes in the area and regulate the allotment of land to members of STs. Problems Suffered by People of Scheduled Areas due to Land Acquisition Land alienation, forced displacement, loss of access and control over forests, due to development projects have been some of the reasons for marginalisation of tribals. This has impacted the lives and health, especially of the Particularly Vulnerable Tribal Groups (PVTGs). They are dependent on forests and are traditionally using its resources for their sustenance but now being evicted from their land for the sake of development, are fighting for their rights. Increasing demands for minerals and land for industrialisation have complicated the issues of tribes. Tribals constitute 8.6 per cent of the Indian population but their contribution to the diversity is immense. In India, there are 227 ethnic groups consisting of 573 tribal communities having six different racial identities—Negroid, Proto-Australoid, Mongoloid, Mediterranean, West Breechy, and Nordic (Rai & Nath). World Bank sociologist, Michael Cernea has researched development induced displacement and resettlement for two decades. Cernea has found eight potential risks intrinsic to displacement (Cernea)—landlessness, joblessness, marginalisation, food insecurity, increased morbidity and mortality, loss of access to common property, and social disintegration. India, keeping pace with the world to provide grassroots level democracy has devolved powers to the local bodies. The legislature of the state has been provided the power to levy, collect and appropriate certain taxes, duties, tolls, fees etc. but these taxes are not sufficient for the Scheduled Areas as most of the population dwelling in these areas are tribals. They don't have much fixed assets and savings; thus, it becomes very difficult for them to start a new living in the rehabilitated area. In the absence of a legal document of their land, the tribals are not able to get loans from formal sources and are left with no other option but to avail loans from non-institutional creditors who charge huge interests. As per household assets and indebtedness survey 2013 conducted by ministry of statistics and programme implementation, about 20 per cent of the households have reported outstanding credit with non-institutional lenders, while the same number is 10 per cent for urban areas.

The Fifth Scheduled Areas have Tribal Advisory Councils (TAC) at the state level which is meant for the debate and discussion for the issues of tribes and to advise the governor of the concerned state. In the original draft of the Fifth Schedule, TACs, were given constitutional power to take up the matters of the tribes residing in Scheduled Areas. Thus, Governor was bound by the advice of the TAC but now it is left to the discretion of the Governor, making it a toothless body.

Low Percentage of Rehabilitation

Only 25 per cent of the total displaced have been rehabilitated during the first three decades of planned development. If we go by data, 2108 families were displaced by the Bhakra Nangal project from the Una and Bilaspur districts of Himachal Pradesh, only 750 have been resettled. Laws made for the protection of tribes are often misused by the local police forces on opposing displacement. Displacement from their original areas according to Xaxa Committee report, 40 per cent of the displaced people are tribes but only 21 per cent of them are rehabilitated. Even when they are not displaced, their livelihood is disturbed as outsiders come in their way. These are the people who settle for that particular development project.

A blatant violation of Article 244 which bans the transfer of tribal land to non-tribals, including companies. In the Hiroli village of Dantewada district of Chhattisgarh, residents have accused the local government of making fake signatures as no Gram Sabha was held for the clearance of an iron ore mining in the area (Subramaniam, 2019). Advent of private players in the projects leads to faster privatisation of the area.

Naxals try to take advantage of this situation and try to increase their influence in these areas. Distressed by government and local authorities, tribals fall prey to Naxalism. Multiple displacement is a major issue. Thirty thousand villagers of Madhya Pradesh were displaced for the first time (late 50s) during the construction of Rihand Dam; again, for the second time when coal was found (mid-70s); third time when an industry was established; and finally, when the Singrauli power plant was mooted (late 80s) (DTE). In another case of fisherfolk families, displaced by New Mangalore Port in 60s, now they are displaced again for Konkan Railway Project.

Panchayats (Extension to Scheduled Areas) Act, 1996 and Issues Associated

On 24th April, 1993, 73rd Constitutional Amendment came into force which inserted Part IX in the Constitution of India. The Act accorded constitutional status to Panchayats, to establish local self-governance for rural India. This provided a structure to the local political system and a sense of representation to people of rural areas. But there is an exception to the implementation of the provisions of Part IX to the Fifth Scheduled Areas, Parliament has the power to extend the provisions of the Part IX with modifications and exceptions. After the 73rd and 74th Amendments of the Constitution, in 1994 Government set up Dileep Singh Bhuria Committee for extending the provisions of 73rd and 74th Amendments to Scheduled Areas. In order to provide special treatment to these areas, government in 1996 enacted a legislation —Panchayats (Extension to Schedule Areas) Act.

This legislation has not only extended the development, planning and audit functioning to the Gram Sabha but has also endowed it with the management and control of natural resources and adjudication of justice in accordance with traditions and customs. Under the legislation, Gram Sabha has been given rights which have mandatory and discretion powers. Gram Sabha has power in the following areas—management of community resources, approve all plans and projects, identification of beneficiaries, issue certificate of utilization of funds. Other rights include—mandatory consultation in land acquisition, resettlement of displaced people, protection of traditional belief and culture, ownership of minor forest products, prevention of land alienation, any other issue arising in case of Scheduled Tribes.

There are various issues with the PESA as it has not been utilized the way it was intended by the policy-makers. Gram Sabha provides citizens a way of participation in policy-making at village level. Each and every one can share their problems and get it solved but the functioning of gram sabhas has not been what it was meant for. Issues such as—low participation, irregular Gram Sabha meetings, absence of a coherent Gram Sabha agendas etc., are major hurdles in its effective functioning. In various instances it is found that people hesitate to give any opinion because they not stand out in terms of financial status in the village. The Sarpanch, elected head of Gram Panchayats exercises significant powers which often prevent others to criticize any programme or project, making Gram Sabhas a symbolic congregation. In case of large irrigation projects, consensus is difficult to arrive at. Dubious land transaction is one of the main reasons of distress among tribals as lack of literacy and awareness of their rights make them vulnerable to fake signatures.

The Act is applicable to the Fifth Scheduled Areas only and does not cover the Sixth Scheduled Areas. Moreover, there are some tribal areas in the country not covered by any of the two schedules. What would be the fate of those tribal people?

While passing the State Panchayat Acts, it should be seen that they are in consonance with the custom, society and religion of the tribals concerned. These aspects vary among tribes within legislation? It may not be possible to have different laws for each tribe within a district or state. Furthermore, the customary laws are not properly codified and documented.

Section 4(b) defines a village as "ordinarily consisting of a habitation or a group of habitations or a hamlet or a group of hamlets comprising a community and managing its affairs in accordance with traditions and customs." It means every community will have a separate village. In a village, several communities may be found spread over different geographical areas. It may be difficult to demarcate a village in this way. In this situation, the revenue village may not be coterminus with the social village. The term 'community' is not clearly defined in the Act and therefore, it would be difficult to delimit a village. This will certainly lead to complications. Usually in tribal areas hamlets are more common than big villages. Therefore, declaring each hamlet as a village panchayat area may not be economically viable.

Under Section 4 (O) of the Act, the Panchayat at the district will be designed PESA and its Implementation on the lines of the autonomous district council under the Sixth Schedule. The ADC has legislative and judicial functions in addition to executive powers (Bijoy, 2013). If only the tribal district panchayats are given legislative and judicial functions, anomalies in the district panchayats within a state will evidently grow. The ADC is empowered to appoint judges for the administration of justice in their areas and they can raise their own police force. These provisions must be examined carefully while extending such powers and authority under the Extension Act. The ADC has limited development functions compared with the Eleventh Schedule to the Constitution. Many states have not devolved powers and functions to panchayats as per the Eleventh Schedule. If the state governments are not willing to devolve powers, authority and responsibilities to local government then the spirit of the 73rd Amendment will be violated.

Reservation of seats has been provided to all communities as per the provisions of Part IX of the Constitution to SCs and STs and one-third of all seats are reserved for women (Vikaspedia, n.d.). Regarding reservation for backward class communities the state legislature must decide. Once again, the term community has been used in its wider sense which includes other than tribal community. When a village is defined on the basis of a community, the question of other communities living in it does not arise. If so, then reservation is only applicable to SCs and in some cases backward classes and also women. Another question is whether Scheduled Castes and women can be considered as communities for reservation purposes.

Under the provisions of the Fifth Schedule, a Tribal Advisory Council (TAC) is to be constituted to advise on matters pertaining to the welfare and advancement of the Scheduled Tribes in the state (Gktoday, 2016). A question arises whether the TAC will obstruct the growth of the Panchayati Raj structure at the local level because if the functional domain of Panchayats is curtailed, they may perceive the TAC as a rival centre. Secondly, the Panchayats will be the creation of the state legislature and to some extent the administrative control over them will be in the hands of the state government. In such a situation will the advice and guidance of the TAC be binding upon the Panchayats? The Panchayats might receive two types of instructions from these two bodies which occasionally may be contradictory. What will be the linkage between TAC and Panchayats? A view is being expressed that when the new dispensation is established, the TAC may become irrelevant. However, if the TAC must continue as only an advisory body what would be the modifications required in its structure and functioning.

Conclusion

There are various issues but the matter of fact remains that tribals conserve the indigenous culture of the area hence it is important to preserve their livelihood. It is well said by Jawaharlal Nehru that—if you are to suffer, you should suffer in the interest of the country. The solution is easy and could easily be taken upon but what is required is the political will. On the whole, the struggle of people and organisation is seeing some hope when the supreme court of the country intervenes. The changing climate is forcing international organisations to be loud sympathisers of tribal issues. Each and everyone should take note of this. For a better future and inclusive growth, tribal land needs to be conserved by each state. Will it be possible to assimilate all types of practices in a single piece of legislation?

References

Aditya, V. (2021, February 24). Displaced from the hills: Livelihoods of tribal communities in Eastern Ghats under threat. *Down To Earth.*

Affairs, M. M. (n.d.). *Land and Governance under Fifth Schedule.* Retrieved from https://tribal.nic.in/downloads/FRA/5.%20Land%20and%20Governance%20under%20Fifth%20Schedule.pdf

Batabyal, A. (1999). Taming the Waters: The Political Economy of Large Dams in India. By Satyajit Singh. Delhi: Oxford University Press, 1997. xiv, 270 pp. $23.95. *The Journal of Asian Studies, 58*(3), 878-79.

Bijoy, C. (2013, February 20). *Panchayat Raj (Extension to Scheduled Areas) Act of 1996: Policy Brief.* Retrieved from UNDP: https://www.in.undp.org/content/india/en/home/library/democratic_governance/UNDP-Policy-Brief-on-PESA.html

Cernea, M. (n.d.). *The Risks and Reconstruction Model for Resettling Displaced Populations.* Retrieved from World bank: https://documents1.worldbank.org/curated/en/909961468740152010/pdf/multi0page.pdf

DTE. (n.d.). *Developing Distress.* Retrieved from *Down To Earth.*

Falak, A. (2018, March 17). *Database for Land Laws Being Created. Sunday Guardian Live.*

Gktoday. (2016, February 24). *Fifth Schedule, Scheduled Areas and Tribal Advisory Council in India.* Retrieved from Gktoday: https://www.gktoday.in/topic/fifth-schedule-scheduled-areas-and-tribal-advisory-council-in-india/

Gogoi, J., Goswami, H., & Borah, K. (2009). *Problems of Border Areas in North East India: Implications for the Thirteenth Finance Commission.* Dibrugarh: Department of Economics, Dibrugarh University. GOI. (n.d.). *Agriculture.* Retrieved from india.gov.in: https://www.india.gov.in/topics/agriculture

GOI. (n.d.). *The Right to Fair Compensation and Transparency in Land Acquisition, Rehabilitation and Resettlement Act,* 2013. Retrieved from INDIA CODE: https://www.indiacode.nic.in/handle/123456789/2121?locale=en

Goswami, A. (2011). Land Acquisition, Rehabilitation and Resettlement: Law and Politics. *India Urban Conference-2011: Evidence and Experience.* Indian Institute for Human Settlement.

India, P. (2015). The Right to Fair Compensation and Transparency in Land Acquisition, Rehabilitation and Resettlement (Amendment) Bill, 2015. PRS. PRS Legislative Research.

Mohanty, A. (2019, May 7). Tribal communities suffer when evicted in the name of conservation. *Down To Earth.*

Portal, I. W. (n.d.). *Development and Displacement.* Retrieved from India Water Portal: https://www.indiawaterportal.org/topics/development-and-displacement

Rai, R., & Nath, V. (n.d.). *The Role of Ethnic and Indigenous People of India and their Culture in the Conservation of Biodiversity.* Retrieved from https://www.fao.org/3/XII/0186-A1.htm

Singh, B. (2019, January 26). The Fifth Schedule of the Constitution- A Critique. Retrieved from *Economic and Political Weekly*: https://www.epw.in/journal/2019/4/perspectives/fifth-schedule-constitution.html

Subramaniam, M. (2019, June 24). *To clear way for mining, did Dantewada administration fake approval from a village council?* Retrieved from Scroll.in: https://scroll.in/article/927611/to-clear-way-for-mining-did-dantewada-administration-fake-approval-from-a-village-council

UN. (n.d.). *Indigenous People at United Nations.* Retrieved from United Nations: https://www.un.org/development/desa/indigenouspeoples/about-us.html

UNESCO. (2018, March 26). *Worsening land degradation impacts 3.2 billion people worldwide.* Retrieved from UNESCO: https://en.unesco.org/news/worsening-land-degradation-impacts-32-billion-people-worldwide

Vikaspedia. (n.d.). Constitutional provisions for development of Scheduled Tribes. Retrieved from *Vikaspedia*: https://vikaspedia.in/social-welfare/scheduled-tribes-welfare/constitutional- provisions-for-development-of-scheduled-tribes

Wahi, N. (n.d.). *Land Rights in Scheduled Areas.*

Yoshino, N., Paul, S., Sarma, V., & Lakhia, S. (2018, July). *Land Acquisition and Infrastructure Development through Land Trust Laws: A Policy Framework for Asia.* Retrieved from ADBI Institute: https://www.adb.org/publications/land-acquisition-and-infrastructure-development-through-land-trust-laws

15

Role of Village Panchayats and Swachh Bharat Abhiyan in Tribal Villages

A Study of Barwani District in Madhya Pradesh

Pushpender Yadav

Introduction

Sanitation and hygiene refer to public health conditions pertaining to uncontaminated drinking and domestic use water with proper treatment and discarding of human excreta in sewage lines. Most important aspect is preventing human contact with faeces to hand washing with soaps and anti-bacterial liquids. The sanitation policies are framed to provide clean environment and healthy life by providing a hygienic environment that stops the transmission of infectious disease through the faecal-oral route. It is fact that individual health and hygiene are largely dependent on proper sanitation and sufficient availability of water for cleanliness. However, sanitation is not a new phenomenon in India, right from the ancient times, importance of sanitation was attached with cleanliness and management of wastages with a system of drainage and waste disposal (Kenoyer, 1988).

India is a fast growing country in the world and indirectly this development is influenced by the well-being of its people related to their hygiene and sanitation practices. This is very clear that India cannot achieve real development if the majority of its rural population resides in unhealthy and unclean surroundings. Sanitation becomes more important where population density is high (Cutler, 2005). The unhygienic conditions and lack of sanitation spread bacterial, viral, parasitic infections, including diarrhoea, polio, cholera and hookworm which deteriorate the health of children and youth (Feachem, 1983).

No doubt India has taken a number of initiatives to improve sanitation system but still situation is not appreciable as compared to developed nations. No doubt that world's fastest growing economies also suffer from inadequate sanitation facilities. United Nations news release revealed that Indians have greater access to mobile phones than to have toilet or improved sanitation facilities inside their houses. The rural sanitation is a serious problem in the country, India is home for 60 per cent of the people who defecate in the open, no doubt there are many sanitation programmes but the rural people resist the behaviour change because they admitted that we feel comfortable in the open fields. It clearly shows that the open defecation is socially acceptable behaviour in rural areas of the country. However, the toilet construction inside the house is acceptable only for young daughters and newlywed daughter-in-laws (Coffey, 2014).

The Constitution of India has not recognized the right to sanitation as fundamental right. However, the Constitution of our country recognizes the right to sanitation indirectly in different form as part of directive principles of the states. The higher judiciary in India (the Supreme Court and High Courts) has interpreted the fundamental right to life under Article 21 of the Constitution.

Sanitation is part of the 'Directive Principles of State Policy' (DPSP) in Part IV of the Constitution. Specifically, part of Article 47 of the Constitution which provides that the government to raise the standard of living. Undoubtedly, a factor that contributes to a decent standard of living. Sanitation is also a part of Article 48A that makes it a duty of the state to 'protect and improve the environment'. The directive principles of the state are not enforceable in the courts and therefore, no individual can approach a court against the government for its failure to provide sanitation to all. (Basu, 2005).

It has been noted that 2.4 billion, or one-third of the world's population continue to remain without improved sanitation in 2015, says a recent World Health Organization and United Nations Children's Fund report. This is a terrible violation of basic human dignity, because clean drinking water and basic sanitation are human rights that impinge on the exercise of other rights. To be sure, the proportion of the population without adequate provision of sanitation decreased from 51 per cent in 1990 to around 33 per cent in 2011 (WHO, 2015). East Asia has registered a 40 per cent increase in sanitation coverage. But recent global progress still falls short of the 2015 Millennium Development Goal (MDG) target to halve the proportion from the 1990 baseline.

The shortfall is in the region of eight per cent, which translates into half a billion people. This relative failure must also be viewed against the significance of the sanitation goal for other targets to minimize the child mortality, improve maternal health, malaria and other diseases. A major cause of concern for public health still remains, with 15 per cent of the world's population practising open defecation. Despite a declining trend from 24 per cent in 1990, the practice is rampant in over a quarter of the population in 27 countries. Water contamination is of particular concern for two reasons. First, while the MDG target relating to drinking water was achieved in 2012, some three-quarters of a billion people continue to rely on unprotected sources. Second, the MDG target on clean water is based on evaluations of the nature of construction of the source, in terms of contamination from the outside, rather than the actual quality of water people consume. Thus, the treatment and disposal of fecal matter are major challenges (B, Madhugopal, 2016).

A study undertaken for India by the Water and Sanitation Programme under the World Bank has estimated the cost of inadequate sanitation for the country's economy at $53.8 billion a year, a figure equivalent to 6.4 per cent of GDP. Among the so-called BRICS (Brazil, Russia, India, China and South Africa) countries, India fares by far the worst, with some 627 million resorting to open defecation. The statistics elsewhere are strikingly small; 14 million in China and half that number in Brazil. The importance of proper sanitation to disaster preparedness can hardly be overstated, given the susceptibility of affected populations to waterborne diseases. Clearly, the universal coverage must remain the core objective, at the level of basic offering of sanitation services and market-based.

According to the Centre on Housing Rights and Evictions, the basic right to sanitation which emphasised that the availability of facilities for the disposal of excreta that should be separate human, animal, and insect contact with excreta. Sewer services, or the emptying of latrines, are another component of adequate sanitation. The U.N. Sub-Commission on the Promotion and Protection of Human Rights has outlined four basic guidelines of the right to sanitation. First, sanitation must be safe, and "conducive to the protection of public health and the environment." This requires a toilet that is hygienic with no risk of collapse and the safe disposal of excreta and wastewater, thereby preventing human, animal, and insect contact. Second, sanitation must be physically accessible within the immediate vicinity of the household or workplace, and that access must not risk the physical safety of the individual. Third, sanitation must be affordable which includes the construction of facilities, emptying and treatment of human waste, and connection to a sewage system without forcing families to sacrifice other basic goods and services. Finally, sanitation must be of a culturally acceptable quality. This encompasses the construction, positioning, and Conditions for use (including separate toilets for men and women), culturally acceptable washing facilities for after toilet use, and a way to empty the latrine which avoids contact with human-waste (Rebbeca, 2011). There are also pay toilets that charge a fee for each use, but these are usually unaffordable for many families living in the slums. No one should be forced to use such alternatives because they are deprived of the safety and dignity of a clean private toilet. Report of Water Aid mentioned that 80 per cent of diseases in the developing world are a result of poor sanitation. Common diseases caused by contact with human waste include dysentery, cholera, typhus fever, typhoid, schistose osmosis, and trachoma (Vishwanathan, Prashanth, 2015). Along with the health and safety risks, the lack of proper sanitation facilities Causes many children to miss school. It is estimated that 443 million school days are lost each year as a result of water-and-sanitation-related diseases. Some healthy children cannot afford school because their family spends scarce financial resources for health services to treat sanitation-related diseases. Even if some children able to attend school, many children are plagued with intestinal worm infections which leave them mentally disabled and incapable of learning. The lack of sanitation disproportionately burden girls' education as they are more frequently absent from school and also assist with household chores, such as fetching water or cleaning latrines. When family members become ill with hygiene-related diseases, the girls of the family are kept at home to take care of them. Beyond their household duties, girls are forced to choose between using a unisex latrine or nothing at all while at school, such a choice causes girls to simply not attend school at all. "This is especially true when young girls reach puberty" (Khurana, 2009). The effects of poor sanitation often result in an economic struggle for poor families. A family expends scarce financial resources for health services to treat sanitation-related diseases instead of spending it on other important needs. According to a study conducted in Karachi, Pakistan, those living in areas without access to sanitation spent six times more on medical treatments than those living with access.

Poor sanitation is costly not only for individual families, but also for the entire country. Sanitation-related diseases drain resources from the public health systems. Profits from tourism wane as travellers are less likely to risk disease by visiting a country with faces-lined streets and an open field as the only toilet. A study by the World Bank found that decreased tourism costs India roughly 260 million dollars annually. Labour productivity also suffers as individuals contract diseases spread through contact with human excreta. It is estimated that over 73 million workdays are lost as a result of waterborne diseases, which translates into an economic burden of 600 million dollars. All factors considered, the World Bank study concluded that a lack of toilets and poor hygiene practices costs India 54 billion dollars every year. This translates into 6.4 per cent of India's gross domestic product (GDP). According to Clarissa Brocklehurst, UNICEF's chief of water, sanitation, and hygiene, India cannot reach its full economic potential unless they do something about this sanitation crisis (*The Economist*, 2014).

Review of Literature

Gong (2015) stated that in recent decades due to rapid economic and urbanization development has become an important trend in developing countries like China. As a result of urbanization large population is concentrating in cities which brought many environmental and sanitation problems, including garbage, dirty streets etc. In 2004, China has surpassed the USA to become the world's largest garbage generator and it clearly shows that workload of sanitation workers is increasing proportionally to urbanization.

In developing countries, sanitation workers are facing job related problems. They are exposed to dust, fumes, harmful materials and chemicals not only this their health and safety are often threatened when they handle hazardous materials. Further, it is emphasised that sanitation workers have little influence over policy formulation and resource allocation at the national and local levels, which makes it difficult for them to improve their access to occupational safety and health. Their interested finding is that there is no national model of pre-job training for sanitation workers in China. The study suggested that we need to raise the awareness of occupational protection of sanitation workers and strengthen research on this vulnerable group in developing countries. Further,

Singh (2014), has depicted in his article that public sanitation is the biggest problem in the county and it covers important aspects of management of human excreta, domestic and industrial wastewater and hazardous substances. The increasing population in the country leaves the policy-makers in puzzle mood that how to provide basic amenities to common people in rural areas where maximum open defecation has been taken place, the mind-set of the people is required to be change and full involvement of educated class of the country for awareness and benefits of cleanliness and healthy environment in context of national development. Further, it is stated that block level administrative and health staff must be responsible for sanitation improvement as per the *modus operandi* of Swachh Bharat Abhiyan in the country.

Govindaswamy (2009) highlighted that sanitation is an integral part of human ecology and it is the responsibility of the state to safe handling of excreta in the human environment. However, the sanitation issue is linked to shyness as the Nobel Laureate Charles Richet has noted that those who wrote on toilet habits are often branded as vulgar and due to this, only a few scholarly documentations exist on this issue.

The report of UNDP (2006) has highlighted that lack of sanitation facilities kills 3900 children on an average daily in Asia. The people in developing countries do not have proper access to toilets and are forced to defecate in the open fields, the governments of these countries have spent billions of dollars in sanitation programmes but results are very limited. These failures are occurred because an inadequate understanding of people's approach to sanitation and they do not have their own toilets. Further, the report has emphasised that controlling sanitation-related diseases is crucial for achieving development goals because health improvements are reported to influence the economic productivity in rural and urban areas.

Further, Jagawat (2005) has clarified that the major part of India's rural development strategy is neglected by catchment areas in remote dry lands where the tribal have lived for centuries.

The sanitation always has been the neglected part in these tribal districts of the country. No doubt the government has started many programmes for sanitation but core target is not achieved yet.

The Planning Commission (2013) study has found that many government schools in Manipur, Assam, Bihar, Meghalaya, Madhya Pradesh and Jharkhand are still without any sanitary facility, many anganwadis are still without toilets even in Nirmal Gram Purushkar (NGP) awarded Gram Panchayats. It is also reported that the scheme of "enhanced rent" for angawadis situated in the private buildings has not delivered the proper and desired results.

Ramani (2016) has depicted in his study that to attract the beneficiaries for construction of toilets and adoption of behaviour change is difficult because of intense competition from television, social media like Facebook and other work of the families. Therefore, to assemble the audience for awareness and education regarding sanitation we need a theatrical, interactive, leaflets, jokes, quizzes, songs, street dramas, movies and entertaining approach for beneficiaries in rural areas.

The National Sample Survey (1998), around 54 samples on sanitation has revealed that the total sanitation programme was promoted as a total package consisting of safe drinking water, scientific disposal of waste water, safe disposal of human excreta including child excreta, solid waste management, food hygiene, personal hygiene and village sanitation. When survey was conducted it has concluded that there has hardly been any significant change in sanitation conditions in rural areas. The survey indicates that only 17.5 per cent of rural population was using toilets. A comprehensive approach is needed to address the rural sanitation problem. If these sanitation problems continue to remain than our future rural generation will remain unproductive due to sanitation-related diseases.

Further, Ramani, V.A. (2015) has stated in his study that till 2005 only two-thirds of the total population has access to any form of functional toilet and deficiency of sanitation coverage has become a major problem. This is not a problem only in India, but at global level, everyday more than 1.1 billion people go for open defecation due to lack of improved sanitation facilities. This huge excreta in the open which is untreated and exposed, becomes the leading cause for spreading diseases. Further, it has been observed that 40 per cent of the world population is suffering without access to appropriate sanitation system. The problem of sanitation is not only of proper provision of appropriate toilet but also of behavioural change of the rural people. So, there is need of new sanitation technological advancement to change the behaviour of rural people.

Further, Singh (2014) has depicted in his article that public sanitation is the biggest problem in the county and it covers important aspects of management of human excreta, domestic and industrial waste water and hazardous substances. The increasing population in the country leaves the policy-makers in puzzle mood that how to provide basic amenities to common people in rural areas where maximum open defecation has been taking place, the mind-set of the people is required to be change and full involvement of educated class of the country for awareness and benefits of cleanliness and healthy environment in context of national development. Further, it is stated that block level administrative and health staff must be responsible for sanitation improvement as per the *modus operandi* of Swachh Bharat Abhiyan in the country.

The Ministry of Drinking Water & Sanitation (2018), a survey was conducted between mid-November 2017 and mid-March 2018, to established baseline with respect to the Disbursement Linked Indicators (DLI) for the World Bank Project to support the Swachh Bharat Mission (Gramin). In this survey, the primary data was collected from the 92,040 households (HH) in 6,136 rural villages across the country, not only households, anganwadis, schools and public community toilets were also surveyed in these villages. The findings of the survey concluded that still people are going for open defecation in the nearby fields. However, their percentage is only 4 per cent. The reasons for this practice is lack of toilet access, lack of water connection inside the toilets, presence of an unhygienic, defunct and unsafe toilet in the house.

Gupta (2016) depicted in their study that despite decade's long toilet construction in rural India open defecation remains a common problem. The reason behind this problem is no change in their behaviour still they prefer to go in open fields for defecation and this is socially acceptable behaviour in rural population. Another important reason for not using toilet is anxieties related to filling of the pit and needs for its cleaning. If we compare the sanitation problems and open defecation of India with the Africa than it is surprising that Africa is nine times as large as India in land area, but the number of people without toilets in India is more than three times that of Africa.

Further, Sanan (2013) has stated in his study that the Government of India has launched many programmes to eradicate the open defecation and sanitation problems from the rural India. These are Central Rural Sanitation Programme (CRSP), 1986, Total Sanitation Campaign (TSC), 1999, Nirmal Bharat Abhiyan (NBA), 2012 and latest one is Swachh Bharat Abhiyan (SBM), 2014. All the sanitation programmes have emphasised on different approaches and methods to free the rural India from open defecation and emphasised on community led total sanitation (CLTS) and to create a triggering environment in the mind of rural people for the toilet demand. Between 2001 and 2011, the Government of India has claimed to have built 78 million toilets in rural areas.

Patil (2014) revealed in their study that open defecation in the agriculture fields is a major cause the persistent problem of diarrhoea and parasite infection in children in rural areas. However, main cause of diarrhoea is open defecation in the rural areas which further contaminated the ground water by mixing with drinking water. Further, it has been observed that most of the studies have been done on the provision of sewerage system in urban areas and very few studies have been done in rural areas where sewerage is prohibitively expensive and neglected. This is the reason that most of the rural sanitation programmes are non-sustainable because of non-networked toilets. So, there is great need to start new projects and research studies to streamline the sewerage problems in rural areas.

Further, Masuki (2015) depicted in his study that in India, there is discrimination against Scheduled Castes and its negative implications for sustainability of sanitation programmes in rural areas. Due to discrimination against sweeper caste and its isolation leads to very low participation from the upper castes in sanitation programmes. However, there is technological advancement in toilet design and flush system but still lot of work needs human involvement. There is need to involve the maximum people from all castes and groups to reduce the open defecation in the rural areas.

Stopnitzky (2016) has stated in his article that Haryana state sex ratios skewed against women and it has been used as social marketing campaign for pro-sanitation messages to households who want to get marry their sons. The pre-condition for marriage of a family from groom side is to construct a toilet inside the house for bride. The slogan used for social marketing campaign was "No Toilet No Bride" and this is surprising that in Haryana private sanitation coverage has increased by 21 per cent and specifically among those households which have boys and they are active in marriage market.

A study by Jain (2016) has clarified that under the SDG (Sustainable Development Goal) sanitation and water are the most important aspects of development because they affect the economic growth and job creation in the world. In India, the progress of sanitation is slow as compare to neighbouring countries like Bangladesh; there is no uniform development in the growth of sanitation coverage all over the country. Sikkim and Himachal have been declared open defecation free but on the other hand like Odisha and Bihar the sanitation coverage is less than 33 per cent in the country.

Research Methodology

The present study is an empirical and descriptive in nature. The primary objective of the study is to measure the impact of the Swachh Bharat Abhiyan (SBA) and grassroots level implementation in rural villages of tribal population. The district Barwani has been selected on the basis of its domination in Scheduled Tribes population. The selected district is further stratified into 2 blocks and 4 villages have been identified for field investigation with 30 households from each village. Purposive sampling method has been used because SBA is runned in all the districts of the state with a total sampled respondents of 4*30=120.

Hypotheses

1. It has been assumed that the availability of water inside the toilets affects its functioning in tribal villages.
2. It is assumed that still rural people are practicing open defecation in tribal rural areas.
3. This has been hypothesized that the females got the maximum benefits of Swachh Bharat Abhiyan in the tribal rural areas.

Sampling Design of the Study

The table given below summarizes the sampling scheme at different levels.

Sample Size

State	District	Name of Blocks	Name of Villages	Sample Size
Madhya Pradesh	Barwani	Barwani	Lonsara Khurd	30
			Taloo-Khurd	30
		Thikri	Bhamori	30
			Bilwa Road	30
Total		**2**	**4**	**120**

The primary data have been collected with the help of semi-structured questionnaires from 4 selected villages in the Barwani district of Madhya Pradesh. Total 120 questionnaires have been prepared to collect the primary data from the sampled households. After the data collection, simple frequencies and a comparative analysis of data have been used with the help of SPSS software to find out the qualitative results.

Table 15.1: Views of sampled respondents regarding availability of water inside their toilets

Barwani					
Thikri	Bhamori		**Frequency**	**Per cent**	**Cumulative Per cent**
		Yes	16	55.2	55.2
		No	12	41.4	96.6
		Can't say	1	3.4	100.0
		Total	**29**	**100.0**	
	Bilwa Road	Yes	15	51.7	51.7
		No	14	48.3	100.0
		Total	**29**	**100.0**	
Barwani	Taloon Khurd	Yes	13	43.3	43.3
		No	14	46.7	90.0
		Can't say	3	10.0	100.0
		Total	**30**	**100.0**	
	Lonsara Khurd	Yes	13	41.9	41.9
		No	17	54.8	96.8
		Can't say	1	3.2	100.0
		Total	**31**	**100.0**	

Table 15.1 reveals that availability of water inside the toilet is an essential component for smooth functioning and cleanliness but it concluded from the above data analysis that almost nearly 50 per cent of the rural households in selected villages are not getting adequate water supply in their toilets, although they have constructed the toilet under the Swachh Bharat Abhiyan. This percentage "54.8 per cent" is highest in the Lonsara Khurd village, followed by Bilwa Road village 48.3 per cent, 46.7 per cent in Taloon Khurd village and 41.4 per cent in the Bamori village. This

has been reported that non-availability of water is the main cause for the failure of toilet functioning in the rural villages, the earlier programme of total sanitation campaign had also faced this problem and not reached to its success level.

Table 15.2: Do you think that people still going for open defecation in your village?

Barwani	Thikri			Frequ-ency	Per cent	Cumul-ative Per cent
		Bhamori	Yes	10	34.5	34.5
			No	6	20.7	55.2
			Can't say	13	44.8	100.0
			Total	**29**	**100.0**	
		Bilwa Road	Yes	20	69.0	69.0
			No	1	3.4	72.4
			Can't say	8	27.6	100.0
			Total	**29**	**100.0**	
	Barwani	Taloon Khurd	Yes	24	80.0	80.0
			No	0	0	80.0
			Can't say	6	20.0	100.0
			Total	**30**	**100.0**	
		Lonsara Khurd	Yes	20	64.5	64.5
			No	2	6.5	71.0
			Can't say	8	29.0	100.0
			Total	**30**	**100.0**	

Table 15.2 highlighted that the open defecation is still a problem in the rural villages as far as data are concerned in the above table that more than 50 per cent of the sampled respondents are agreed that still people are going for open defecation in the open fields nearby the villages. The open defecation is highest with 80.0 per cent in Taloo Khurd village, 69.0 per cent in Bilwa Road village, 64.5 per cent in Lonsara Khurd village and 34.5 per cent in Bhamori village. The basic objective of Swachh Bharat Abhiyan

was open defecation free villages but still people are practicing open defecation which needs more intervention approach to change the behaviour of the people for using the toilets.

Table 15.3: Do you think female got benefit from toilet under the Swachh Bharat Abhiyan?

Barwani	**Thikri**			**Frequ-ency**	**Per cent**	**Cumulative Per cent**
		Bhamori	Yes	25	86.2	86.2
			No	2	6.9	93.1
			Can't say	2	6.9	100.0
			Total	**29**	**100.0**	
		Bilwa-Road	Yes	22	75.9	75.9
			No	3	10.3	86.2
			Can't say	4	13.8	100.0
			Total	**29**	**100.0**	
	Barwani	Taloon-Khurd	Yes	23	76.7	76.7
			No	2	6.7	83.3
			Can't say	5	16.7	100.0
			Total	**30**	**100.0**	
		Lonsara-Khurd	Yes	26	83.9	83.9
			No	1	3.2	87.1
			Can't say	4	12.9	100.0
			Total	**31**	**100.0**	

Table 15.3 revealed that the majority of the beneficiaries that triggers for toilet construction under the Swachh Bharat Abhiyan are females. This percentage is highest with 86.2 per cent in Bhamori village in Thikri tehsil followed by the 83.9 per cent in Lonsara Khurd, 76.7 per cent in Taloo-Khurd and 75.9 per cent Bilwa Road village. The role of village panchayats in these four villages has been well coordinated and use of community groups played very important role for the maximum awareness among the females to raise the demands for toilet construction. The maximum

uses of toilets are also used by the females as they faced lot of problems such as privacy and dignity.

Policy Implications

Rural sanitation is an important parameter for the healthy life of rural population in tribal villages which further contributes to nation's development. The rural people still need more awareness and clarity about the use of human excreta as manure in the agriculture fields and other health benefits of toilet use. At last it has been concluded that the Swachh Bharat Abhiyan (Gramin) is one of the best sanitation programmes which is directly improving the health conditions of the children, women and men in the rural tribal dominated population areas in Madhya Pradesh, let's do more emphasis on people's participative approach and adopt the water harvesting approach in rural areas to make this campaign a successful one. Apart from the people's participation approach in the rural sanitation, the concerned state government must take steps to provide water pipe line connections in the rural households of villagers as the data in Table 15.1 reveals that water is the biggest issue for the survival of toilets under the Swachh Bharat Abhiyan. Secondly, no doubt there has been progress in behaviour change of the rural people to use the toilets for defecation but the data shown in Table 15.2 highlights that still people are going for open defecation which is against the hygienic conditions and it will encourage the children to go in open for defecation, the government must take initiative to stop it with the help of rural people, district and block level officials. Thirdly, the state government must intervene in the working of administrative staff at the block level as it has been concluded from the finding in Table 15.3 that there has been very less participation of block level officials to monitor and supervise the Swachh Bharat Abhiyan in the villages. Now, toilets have been constructed in all the villages but still administrative intervention needed for the sustainability of constructed toilets, also monitoring should be done after the one year of construction to check the status of toilets. Lastly, it has been recommended that

Swachh Bharat Abhiyan is not over yet, we have to continue with the good practices of hygienic and proper treatment of waste water to make tribal villages free from open defecation.

Acknowledgements

The author acknowledges the initiative and assistance provided by the Indian Council of Social Sciences (ICSSR) for the work on Swachh Bharat Abhiyan in Madhya Pradesh. Also thankful to Indian Institute of Public Administration (IIPA) for providing mean opportunity to prepare an article on the relevance of water in the sustainability of Swachh Bharat Abhiyan.

References

B. Madhugopal (2016, June 24). "Towards a Cleaner Railway Stations. Modern Green Toilets Being Constructed Near Entrance". Vishakhapatnam, Andhra Pradesh, India: *The Hindu.*

Basu, D. (2005). *Introduction to the Constituion of India.* New Delhi: Lexus & Nexis.

Coffey, E. (2014). "Revealed Preference for Open Defecation: Evidance from a New Survey in Rural North India". *Economic & Political Weekly*, 43-55.

Cutler, D. (2005). "The Role of Public Health Imoprovements in Health Advances: The Twentieth Century—United States". *Demography*, 1-22.

Feachem, R. (1983). *Sanitation and Disease: Health Aspect of Excreta and Waste Water Management: World Bank Studies on Water Supply and Sanitation.* Washington DC: World Bank.

Gong, Y. (2015). "Occupational safety and health status of sanitation workers in urban areas: A piolt study of wuhan China". *International Journal of Occupational Safety and Ergonomics*, 435-442.

Govindaswamy, A. (2009). "India Needs Sanitation Policy Reforms to Enhance Public Health". *Journal of Economic Policy Reforms*, 333-342.

Gupta, A. (2016). *Understanding Open Defecation in Rural India: Untouchability, Pollution & Latrine Pits.* London: International Growth Centre, London School of Economics, University of Oxford.

Jagawat, H. (2005). *Transforming the Dry Land: The Sadguru Story of Western India.* New Delhi: India Resarch Press.

Jain, A. (2016). *Is India Winning War Against Open Defecation*? New Delhi: NITI Ayog.

Kenoyer, J.M. (1988). *Ancient Cities of the Indus Civilization.* Oxford: American Institute of Social Studies.

Khurana, I. (2009). *Towards Understanding the Rights to Water and Sanitation.* New Delhi: Dhanpat Rai Publisher.

Masuki, Y. (2015). "The Role of Civil Society for Community Development in Contemporary India: A Case of an NGO for the Sweeper Caste in Rajasthan". *Procedia Environmental Science*, 106-114.

Ministry of Drinking Water & Sanitation. (2018). *National Annual Rural Sanitation Survey* (NARSS) 2017-18. New Delhi: India Environment Portal.

National Sample Survey (1998). *54th Round on Common Property Resources, Sanitation and Hygiene Services.* New Delhi: National Sample Survey.

Patil, E. (2014). *The Effects of India's Total Sanitation Campaign on Defecation Behaviour and Child Health in Rural Madhya Pradesh.* Madhya Pradesh: Bill Gates & Milinda Gates Foundation.

Planning Commission (2013). *Evaluation Study on Total Sanitation Programme.* New Delhi: Planning Commission, Government of India.

Ramani, V.A. (2016). "Catalysing Innovation for Social Impact: The Role of Social Enterprises in Indian Sanitation Sector". *Technological Forecasting & Social Change*, 1-15.

Ramani, V.A. (2015). *Ending Open Defecation—Doing it Properly: SDG 6. 17 Days & 17 Goals* (pp. 1-2). New York: United Nations University.

Rebbeca, M. (2011). "Human Rights of Sanitation for all: A Study of India". *Global Business & Law Journal*, 1-10.

Sanan, D. (2013). "Adopting Nirmal Bharat Abhiyan Policy for Improved Outcomes". *Making the Nirmal Bharat Abhiyan an Effective Instrument for Total Sanitation* (pp. 1-25). Uttarakhand: Nainital.

Singh, M.K. (2014). "Sanitation in Rural India". *International Journal of Research in Humanities Arts and Literature*, 19-24.

Stopnitzky, T. (2016). *No Toilet No Bride.* San Francisco, USA: University of San Francisco.

The Economist. (2014, July 19). *The Economist.* Retrieved September 16, 2021, from economist.com: Retrieved from https://www.economist.com/asia/2014/07/19/the-final-frontier

UNDP. (2006). "Beyond Scarcity Power, Poverty and Global Water Crisis", *Human Development Report.* New York: United Nations Human Development Report.

Vishwanathan, Prashanth (2015, March 10). *Water Aid.* Retrieved September 16, 2021, from wateraidindia.in: Retrieved from https://www.wateraidindia.in/themes-of-our-work

WHO (2015). *Millennium Development Goals.* Geneva: World Health Organization.

Index